MANAGEMENT DECISION SYSTEMS

MANAGEMENT DECISION SYSTEMS
Computer-Based Support for Decision Making

MICHAEL S. SCOTT MORTON
Associate Professor of Management
Alfred P. Sloan School
Massachusetts Institute of Technology

Formerly Research Assistant in Business Administration
Harvard University

DIVISION OF RESEARCH
GRADUATE SCHOOL OF BUSINESS ADMINISTRATION
HARVARD UNIVERSITY
BOSTON · 1971

Library of Congress Catalog Card No. 72–132152
ISBN 0–87584–090–6

PRINTED IN THE UNITED STATES OF AMERICA

Table of Contents

LIST OF EXHIBITS

List of Figures

FOREWORD

THIS BOOK IS OF INTEREST because of its contrast with the current state of published work in the Management Information Systems field in universities. The last five years have been singularly short of academic experimentation in the MIS field. There has been some good laboratory work, but almost nothing in the way of field experiments. Without active disciplined exposure to real managers in a real setting, the MIS area will be unable to develop viable hypotheses. This book reports one field experiment. It should be of interest not only to academicians but also to managers. It reports a method by which executives can gain insight into decision problems with only a modest expenditure of capital.

A further contribution lies in the author's willingness to take a new piece of technology, develop a perspective on its role in the MIS field, and then go ahead and actually implement a realistic working system for use in an experiment. All too often new technology is discussed extensively but few, particularly in the universities, get involved in the discouraging but real problems of building and testing systems that incorporate the new technology and attack a real problem.

The potential power of the kinds of systems discussed in this book is real. Businessmen and researchers must develop the perspective necessary to understand where and when this power can usefully be applied. Our history, as a country, has been shaped by our willingness to absorb new ideas. In recent years there has been a tendency toward the "bandwagon" effect on people and on the reactions of companies to new ideas and new issues. This has certainly been true in the use of computers in organizations. The potential impact is undeniably there, but in the initial rush of enthusiasm for the technique the force has been lost or misapplied.

More research is needed similar to that reported here, conducted either by academic institutions or by companies, if we are to capture the power inherent in the recent surge of new technology.

The product of this research is the result of an extensive commitment by the company involved throughout this final research effort. Several of the company's executives gave their energy, time, and attention, in addition to their normal responsibilities, to fulfill this commitment. This spirit of cooperation is vital to the creation of productive research in the managerial decision process. Computer systems research, particularly, is heavily dependent upon field environments, as we endeavor to better understand how such complex systems will influence both the behavior of the individual and the overall architecture of the organization. The management community owes a debt of gratitude to this company and all of its executives for their time and investment in this effort. In addition, the Harvard Business School provided some financial assistance made possible by the income of an endowment fund for research which came from an anonymous donor.

In some sense, this volume produces a significant landmark in the mass of data published on the "influence of the computer on the manager." All too often such comments are the basis of someone's own experience or intuition of the process as he perceives it from his particular niche. Further, not an insignificant portion of those materials are based more on what people desire to obtain or hope will occur. Professor Morton is to be commended for creating a sound example of how to consider the "influence." This work is in the tradition of careful field research and demonstrates its applicability to the expanding field of computer systems.

JAMES L. MCKENNEY
Professor of Business Administration
Director of Computer Services
Harvard Business School

Soldiers Field
Boston, Massachusetts
June 1970

Preface

THE PRIMARY FOCUS OF THE WORK IN THIS BOOK is on the impact
that Management Decision Systems have on the manager's problem-solving process. It is not focused on display devices or software
design. Management Decision Systems is, in a sense, a point of
view, and in this case includes interactive terminals, careful
analysis of key decisions, a supporting data-base, and a model base.
The impact of these components on a certain class of problem is
described in some detail.

The origin of this book lies in the dissatisfaction I felt as a
student reading the material on the impact of computer technology
on management. This material fell into two camps: the yes-man-
agement-will-be-revolutionized group, or the no-they-will-not-be-
affected group. The literature was full of dogmatic assertions but
there was very little straightforward observation and assessment.
People seemed too busy implementing systems to think very much
about what they were doing.

The work described in this book almost fell into this trap of
letting the task of building it become an end in itself. Although
the initial question was "what impact will interactive display
systems have on management decision making," the effort of
building the system very nearly turned the experiment into one
that tested whether you *could* build such systems and have managers use them. There is interesting work to be done on interactive
software design for such systems, but the major problems to be
solved lie in the area of understanding how to provide useful,
active support for managers.

The underlying issue, therefore, is *not* can managers use such
systems, but rather, when and under what conditions are such
systems useful. To repeat, the issue of whether or not managers

can use interactive terminals is not as interesting a question as the central problem of the conditions under which the use of interactive terminals will be of benefit to a manager. The question of matching the problem type to the relevant technology is extremely important. This book discusses the kinds of problems, the sort of technology, and the type of analysis that must go on before such systems can be built. It continues with the central theme of the influence of the computer system on management decision making. In order to document and understand this innovation, over two years were spent observing the behavior of a decision-making team in its planning and controlling of a production-marketing system. The team was observed at the beginning of the research as it allocated resources and set a pattern of schedules. Then, after analysis, an on-line computer system with graphical capability was developed to aid the team's decision-making activities. The team was observed again as it used the system for support in its planning and control decisions. The decision processes, the impact, and the nature of the experimental system are all described in enough detail to allow the reader to see the impact of such systems on managers dealing with this general class of problem.

This book is based on my doctoral dissertation written in partial fulfillment of the requirements of the degree of Doctor of Business Administration, Harvard University, 1967. Considerable help was provided by my thesis committee in the definition and clarification of all the issues faced in the thesis entitled "Computer Driven Visual Display Devices: Their Impact on the Management Decision-Making Process." Professor James L. McKenney bore the brunt of endless drafts and half-formed ideas and was of immeasurable assistance in helping with the formulation of the topic and the design. Professors John Dearden and Lewis B. Ward read, criticized, and offered significant help with the original experimental design. I am also grateful to Professor Bertrand Fox, formerly Director of the Division of Research, for his encouragement and support in making this publication possible, and to the Sloan School of Management, Massachusetts Institute of Technology, for the time I have spent completing the manuscript and making it ready for publication. This book benefits from all of their efforts. Despite this most generous help and guidance of the persons mentioned above, I must accept full responsibility for the contents of the final manuscript.

It was important for this project to take place in a live organization. The company's willingness to fund this R&D effort to the extent they did was central to its success. Only with the active participation of a competent group of managers, management systems, and computer professionals could we have overcome the myriad problems that surrounded the use of an early implementation of a new form of technology.

This book describes an experiment. Since its completion there have been a number of others in a similar vein that have been run from the Sloan School of Management at MIT. Other business schools and a few companies are also active in this field. By this experimentation with different equipment and different settings we will be able to build up a good understanding of this new field of Management Decision Systems.

This research, then, describes the first of what will be a long series of experiments that will help us to understand how to build support systems for management decision making. It is an exciting field, one that is with us technologically but one that we have barely begun to utilize in ongoing organizational settings. The research potential is enormous and the challenge very clear.

Michael S. Scott Morton

Cambridge, Massachusetts
June 1970

MANAGEMENT DECISION SYSTEMS

Chapter 1

THIS BOOK, CONCERNED WITH MANAGEMENT DECISION SYSTEMS (MDS), is based on research using a combination of interactive visual display terminals, computers, and analytical models. The approach focuses on an analysis of key decisions and then the provision of support to managers in making these key decisions. This support is possible in complex, unstructured, problem situations and can be used by the manager in conjunction with his intuitive "feel" for the problem and its solution. The background for this approach is an experiment in which managers were actually involved in using the system in an operating environment.

Computer technology has advanced at a rapid rate but thus far has had little, if any, direct impact on managerial action. Recent developments with computers which are able to drive several remote terminals, plus the work with new forms of display terminals, have resulted in a new form of technology available at reasonable cost. More particularly, this new technology offers the possibility of coupling the manager, at any level and in any environment, with information and decision-making support from the computer. These technological advances, then, call for a shift in thinking by managers and systems designers at least as radical as that required when computers were first introduced at the functional level in the late 1950s.

As the technology changes, it seems reasonable that there should be some changes in management's traditional planning and control systems. With the increasingly complex and rapidly moving business world, it becomes important for managers to shift as much as is feasible of their structured tasks to the machine. In addition, research into formal planning, simulation models, and other analytical techniques suggests that we have reached a point where these could usefully be integrated into the ongoing decision process.

The material in this book identifies the potential in this field and presents some evidence of the impact of such systems on the managers' decision-making process. The corporation setting in which this research took place, the design process, and the changes in managerial behavior are all discussed in the following chapters in an attempt to provide some overview and a feeling for the likely impact of this new approach on the modern corporation.

This project, then, is concerned with managerial use of a visual display system to support decision making. The company involved is a large firm with about 70 divisions manufacturing a range of products that runs from electric toothbrushes to industrial turbines. The divisions are organized on a profit-center basis and are located throughout the United States. This study is concerned with the divisions that manufacture and sell laundry equipment, that is, washing machines and dryers. There has been a long tradition of innovation with computer technology in this company but the particular divisions, and their management in this experiment, are not significantly different from others in their industry as far as their background and previous use of computer technology is concerned.

The problem selected for this experiment is typical of problems involving middle-level and senior managers. Those involved in the initial experiments were the marketing manager, the production manager, and the market planning manager. The marketing manager was responsible for the entire country and reported directly to the manager in charge of the sales division, which was responsible for all consumer products. The production manager reported directly to the division manager. The market planning manager held a staff position designed to provide planning support for the sales division manager. Every month the company had to make plans for the manufacture, sales, and distribution of their laundry products. These short-term and intermediate-term decisions involved the areas of marketing (promotion, advertising, and pricing decisions), as well as production (scheduling, purchasing, work force levels, and similar problems). In addition, the inventory levels and customer service requirements had to be balanced for normal operations and also geared up to support special sales activities. This complex set of interacting variables provided a planning problem of considerable difficulty. The profitability of the divisions was heavily influenced by the quality of these decisions, and opportunities existed for considerable losses as well as dramatic profits.

The experiment involved detailed problem analysis followed by the construction of a system which used an interactive visual display terminal, access to models, and a relevant data-base. The terminal was available to the managers at the corporate headquarters. The computer, related systems software, and data-base were located about 15 miles away and were connected to the terminal via regular telephone lines.

The managers were observed in the decision process before and after the introduction of the management decision system. This initial experiment, with these two series of observations, provided the material for some generalizations as to the impact of the system.

There has been considerable expansion and experimentation with the system since this first experiment was completed, and some of these points are raised in the final chapter. The impact discussed here is that of the first experiment. A number of organizational changes have taken place since then, but the basic findings have been found to hold in the larger use of the system since the experiment, which was completed two years ago.

With this amount of use the results may be of interest to practicing managers as well as the management systems, research, and academic communities.

GOALS OF THE PROJECT

Computer-driven visual display devices have an immediate appeal. In operation they look immensely impressive; the speed, silence, and complicated displays that are possible all combine to indicate a powerful new tool. Graphics for engineering design work and the vast array of military applications have insured that the manufacturers will continue to produce such devices. The sight of the engineer or scientist at work on his graphics console provides a clear demonstration that man/machine communication is possible in some fields. One of the basic questions that is explored in this study is whether such systems have a role in the management process, and if so, where?

The first goal of this project was to see if it was possible to use a visual display system in a management setting. The second goal was to obtain some evidence on where in the management ranks such a device might be used and, more importantly, on what classes of problems the system could be used most effectively. This approach ignores the difference between whether a manager personally used the system or whether he had his staff use it, although in this particular instance the managers involved normally used the system themselves.

The third goal of the project was to determine what impact such a device would have on the decision-making process. Care was taken to avoid the trap of saying such a device would *improve* the decision-making process. What the project did show was that the device *affected* the decision-making process and it specified what these effects were. The reader is left to decide whether he would find the device useful or not, but he is given the users' subjective views of their recommendations concerning the utility of the system.

These goals necessitated the use of a visual display device in an ongoing management setting. A real manager with a real problem was a necessary prerequisite. As a result, this research project suffers from the lack of clinical detachment which is possible in a laboratory with true "ceteris paribus" conditions. Nevertheless, the results seem to be sufficiently clear that this disadvantage is outweighed.

Project Rationale

The reasons for undertaking this project were in many ways more important than the specific goals. There were four such reasons all of which are derived from the belief that the powerful techniques of management science can make a great difference to the performance of managers, and thus companies. Yet management science techniques have hardly begun to touch the life of a typical manager. The opportunities for the application of scientific decision making are enormous, and the payoffs most rewarding. Interactive terminal systems appear to have the capability of bringing these techniques closer to the manager who has the judgment to interpret the results. For the reasons that follow, an important contribution can be made by providing the manager with a tool that will make him more effective in his utilization of his scarcest resource—time.

Management Planning and Control

One of the basic rationales for this work was the belief that events in the environment, and the marketplace, of the modern corporation are moving at a faster pace than before, and that managers have to develop planning and control techniques to match. In many companies the size of a manager's responsibilities is much larger than in years past, but in all cases the tempo of his job is faster.[1] Because of changes in the marketplace, competition, mergers or technological change, every company has to have an evolving management planning and control system if it is to survive in the most profitable way.

One possible way of improving a manager's ability to plan and control is to provide him with some of the capability possessed by large-scale computers. We may, in fact, be reaching the point where the manager *in combination* with the computer is going to be a significantly different and more effective manager than one without the computer. Of course, the computer is *not* the essence of management planning and control but, at the same time, it is far from clear whether or not the manager *alone* will be able to exercise effective control in the years to come.

Providing managers with facts (as opposed to raw data) is not a simple matter. The assumption is, first of all, that the problem

---

[1] Robert Anthony, Leatherbee Lectures, 1967 (16). The figures in parentheses refer to the numbered items in the Bibliography at the end of this book.

confronting the manager is adequately defined, indeed has been discovered, and further that the data are in forms that will be useful. It is the terminal system's ability to provide flexible access to the data-base, model-bank, and manipulative capability of the computer that allows it to be used in an interactive manner by the manager. It seems that such access might permit problem *definition* as well as problem *solution* activity. It was, in part, in an effort to see whether this could occur that this research was undertaken.

Management Problem Solving

A second reason for undertaking this project was to explore the possibilities for improvement in human problem solving. Observation of managers at work indicates that they spend a large portion of their time in verbal communication with others. This is also true within a decision-making cycle; that is, the process of defining and solving problems is often accomplished by "talking" the problem through to solution.

The internal and very informal "model," or set of guidelines, that each manager has in his mind is used by him as a frame of reference against which to pass the facts that he perceives in a conversation. From this, and other sources, he develops his definition of a problem—that is, a difference between what his internal "model" says is expected and what he actually perceives. Similarly, he has informal models or processes that he uses to solve problems as he perceives them. In both cases the problem finding and problem solving are intuitive judgmental kinds of processes.

It seems desirable to leave the manager with this freedom but also to help him build as firm a base from the facts as possible—and only then have him apply his judgment to this base. This is done by providing him with flexible access to the data and by making available the use of relevant formal models to process and filter the data for him. There is a rapidly expanding technology in the field of Operations Research and mathematical models. This technology can be brought to bear on problems and made to support the manager's decision. The computer technology and the modeling technology will allow this, and it is clear that this technology can be used by normal line managers with considerable benefit.

Computers and Management

It is important to have some framework in which to think of management decision making, otherwise we cannot assess the impact of computers so far. Nor can we predict the future development of the framework of computers and their use in the actual process of decision making, discussed in Chapter 3. One way of thinking of the broader setting of classes of management decisions is to combine the two schemes suggested by Anthony[2] and Simon.[3] Anthony specifically rules out Cells 2, 3, and 4 in Exhibit 1–1. However, it is useful for our purposes not to be quite so rigorous.

EXHIBIT 1–1

CATEGORIES OF MANAGEMENT DECISION MAKING

	Operational Control	Management Control	Strategic Planning
Structured	1	2	3
Unstructured	4	5	6

Simon, in distinguishing between structured and unstructured problems, talks of the former as being well-defined, and repetitive, a decision for which rules or algorithms exist. By unstructured he means a decision that is hazy, vague, and ill-defined. These are not precisely defined by him, but for our purposes here they can be thought of as two ends of a continuum of problem structure.

Anthony claimed that all decisions made within a firm fall into one of three categories: strategic planning, management control, and operational control.[4]

(1) Strategic planning is the process of deciding on objectives of the organization, on changes in these objectives, on the resources used to attain these objectives, and on the policies that are to govern the acquisition, use, and disposition of these resources.

---

2 See Anthony (3).
3 See Simon (72).
4 Anthony (3), pp. 16–18.

(2) Management control is the process by which managers assure that resources are obtained and used effectively and efficiently in the accomplishment of the organization's objectives.

(3) Operational control is the process of assuring that specific tasks are carried out effectively and efficiently.

He argues that these are points on a continuum and that the boundaries are fuzzy, but that these are the major classes involved.

Examples of structured operational control might be inventory control decisions, payroll and other financial accounting matters, and so forth. Unstructured operational control decisions might be job-shop scheduling, decisions about where to invest the company's large cash balance for two-day and three-day periods and other repetitive decisions that have to do with daily operations for which as yet no good rules have been developed.

Examples of structured management control decisions might be the variance analysis process of the budget or the execution of many personnel policies. Unstructured decisions in this category might be the budget-setting process, or determining the levels and programs involved.

Strategic planning decisions that have proved to be at least partly structured are those concerned with warehouse or new factory location, tanker fleet mix, and other problems that have proved tractable with large simulation models or optimizing techniques. Unstructured decisions, of course, are those similar to new product possibilities or mergers and acquisitions.

These are merely examples to illustrate the general meaning of this classification scheme. Computers so far have had almost all of their impact in Cells 1 and 2 with some in 3 (see Exhibit 1–1), and virtually none elsewhere.

From a management standpoint this current status of computer use is significant, as almost all interesting and important management problems lie in Cells 3, 4, and 5 (Exhibit 1–1). As has been pointed out by others,[5] the impact of computers on management has not been as large as many of its initial prophets predicted.[6] There is no question that the computer could be of greater help to managers in their decision-making tasks even though most

[5] See Dearden (22).
[6] See Diebold (24).

managers deal with dynamic unstructured problems a good deal of the time. If they are unstructured, if indeed the problem itself is often unknown, then all that is visible to the manager are a few clues. In addition, management problems are typically dynamic ones, changing from month to month. It is therefore difficult to have a formal system set up to provide information for their solution. The last thing most managers would consider doing is to call in a computer programmer and set up a system to provide information to monitor one particular situation. By the time the computer program was finished, there would be a new problem in some other area. For instance, inventory levels of certain products are a problem in one month, then perhaps pricing activity of the competition will be a major issue in the next. To obtain the services of a systems analyst, develop with him the report one needs, and then perhaps wait for weeks while he develops a program on a batch-processing computer is not often a feasible solution. As a result of this inflexibility with batch-processing computers and their systems, many managers continue to rely on intuition or manual information systems. In short, the setup costs are too high, and the response time too slow for much meaningful managerial use of batch-processing computers in dynamic unstructured problem areas.

This sort of phenomenon explains the great appeal of some form of interaction, with the computer, its data-base and models, that allows for problem finding and problem solution in unstructured problem areas—a system easy for the manager to use, that lets the machine do those things at which it is best and allows man to provide the heuristic capability, the insight. The notion of flexible interaction, allowing the manager to ask a broader range of specific questions, has considerable appeal. He can follow up on his hunches, try out a plan, make a point to his superior or subordinate—all of this done quickly enough so that it is natural and easy for him. If such a system is feasible, then it seems reasonable that it might have some use. This point has been ably expressed by many others, of which Sprague,[7] Carroll,[8] and Zannetos[9]

---

[7] See Sprague (76).

[8] See Carroll (10).

[9] See Zannetos (86, 87).

are perhaps the principal exponents. Such a combination has never actually been tried in a business setting except in simple structured situations.[10] For this reason, it seemed that an attempt to do so was overdue, particularly since in much of the discussion to date the manager who is actually going to use the system has not been approached for an opinion. This study used responsible managers, without extensive computer experience; indeed they had never even heard of visual display devices. The managers involved form a small sample of three, but at least they have helped to provide some evidence as to the feasibility and desirability of using such a system.

Technical Alternatives

The final reason for undertaking this study was the paucity of information, available to the technological world, that could provide guidelines for hardware and software development.

The field of interactive computing is so new that there has been little experience and even less research. Interactive computing for management is virtually nonexistent in the real world. We need to understand both the human problems (those of the user) and the hardware problems, if progress is to be made. We require hard data on what the machine can and should do, and what is economical and desirable for the man to do. In short, we need answers in all of the following areas:

(1) Software requirements for interactive terminals.
(2) Nature of the interface between manager and device.
(3) Central computer requirements to support terminals.
(4) Problem characteristics to which the system can be applied.
(5) Type of user able to work with the system.

The research reported here provides one datum point in the long process of collecting evidence from which to build theory in these five technical areas. The discussion that follows does not prove any points or provide generalizable evidence on the issues involved, but it is a start.

The work, therefore, was undertaken for the four major reasons:

---

[10] See Morton (49).

to provide some evidence on the issues involved with management planning and control; management problem solving; computers and management; and technical alternatives. This was done in an attempt to collect some evidence on the advantages and disadvantages of interactive terminal systems in a management setting. Despite the need for a great deal more research, the evidence is strong enough to suggest that our concepts and the technology are able to support new forms of planning and control systems.

OVERVIEW OF MAJOR RESULTS

The previous discussion has outlined the nature of the experiment and study. The sections below discuss the five major categories of impact that the Management Decision System (MDS) had on the managers involved. This brief discussion provides an overview of the types of impact that might be expected when such a system is used to assist managers in solving complex unstructured problems of this type.

Operational Use

The most interesting aspect of the study, in many respects, is that the MDS was in operational use. That is, responsible executives preferred to use the MDS for their planning problems, rather than their previous methods. In their minds the MDS allowed them to develop better decisions in a shorter time period. In point of fact there is no certain way of showing in general that the decisions are "better." At the very least, several years of use would be required before arriving at even a tentative general conclusion as to clear improvement in decision making. However, in the comments that follow, particularly in Chapters 7, 8 and 9, it is clear that the MDS does have an *impact* on the decision-making process.

The managers involved used the MDS on a regular basis. Thus, we can conclude that it is possible for managers to solve certain classes of problem with the MDS even though they have no technical knowledge in the computer field. In other words, a manager with no knowledge, or interest, in computers, or file structure, or similar technical details can find visual display systems and computer-based models and data useful means of problem solving. This is significant, because the problem that the managers were working on cannot possibly be solved well by the computer alone. Neither can it be solved well by the managers alone, as demonstrated by the complexity of the problem, discussed in Chapter 4. This is not a simple information retrieval situation or some other "programmed" problem. Management judgment of a high order is involved, and many hundreds of thousands of dollars of profit, or loss, ride on these decisions.

With the use that these nontechnically trained managers made of the system, it is clear that a *man/machine combination is possible*. Such a combination can be used on complex problems in an unstructured problem-solving environment. In addition, these particular managers claimed that the MDS improved decision making as well as shortened the decision-making cycle, particularly by allowing them to look forward in time and test various alternatives rather than forcing them to deal with masses of historical data.

Impact on Time

The changed time scale has several important effects; in fact, it is the underlying cause for many of the impacts discussed in Chapters 7 and 8. However, it is important to distinguish between the different kinds of time involved. The three types of time effect discussed below are separated in order to highlight the difference between the accessibility and the currency of the information. The MDS gave the managers immediate *access* to the data-base and manipulative power. Both of these allowed an interactive method of problem solving. The currency, or age, of the data-base is irrelevant as long as it is adequate for the purpose at hand. In this situation the data-base contained monthly information and was at least four days "old" by the time it was used. However, it was adequate for the purpose. This implies that the data-base can be updated as appropriate, and does not have to be updated in "real-time," a significant saving in cost.

Contact Time

With the MDS the amount of time spent by the manager actually working with the problem was sharply reduced. In this case the reduction was by a factor of 12 to 1. The length of time spent actually working on the problem in order to arrive at a solution was reduced from six days to half a day.

Assuming that the managers are in responsible positions and have complex problems, it is reasonable to suppose that the free time now available will be put to good use. Ideally, some portion of it might go to planning and further improvement of the problem-solving process.

Regardless of the precise use these managers make of the extra time, it is clear that it exists and *could* be put to profitable use.

Elapsed Time

Chapter 7 points out that the elapsed time also changed significantly—from 22 days to 1 day. The length of time between starting and finishing the problem-solving process affects the quality of the final decision. If there are two or three days between meetings, then most of the time in the meeting is spent establishing where one was at the end of the previous session, and so forth. Similarly, it is unlikely that many of the nuances of the situation are remembered from one session to another. Hence, they have to be regenerated each time.

In addition to this, as time passes, the information on which decisions are being based is increasingly less current, and the decision may suffer as a result.

Under the MDS, none of these disadvantages appear, as the elapsed time is short. To the extent that the delay adversely affects the quality of the decision under the old process, then the new process (MDS) is an improvement.

Response Time

As was mentioned above, it is important that the speed of response of the on-line system be kept distinct from the currency of the data-base. There is no necessity in this application to have "real-time" information. That is, the information being used can be, indeed was, several days "old" when the decision-making process started. Monthly data from the previous month were used, starting on the third or fourth working day of the following month. However, the *response* to a managerial request had to be immediate if the decision process was not to be impeded. With the MDS on-line to the computer the response time to a request was immediate. This was responsible for keeping both the contact and the elapsed time low. More important, it allowed the managers to develop an interactive mode of problem solving. This interaction changed the whole structure of their decision-making process.

It may be economically desirable, for other reasons, to maintain and collect their data on-line in real-time (OLRT), as in fact this company did, but this is a separate issue and can be decided separately. The use of an MDS does not *necessarily* mean that the data-base has to be maintained on a continuing operational basis on an OLRT system. However, the use of an MDS does mean that the terminal has to be on-line and the *response during* the problem-solving phase must be in real-time.

Problem Finding

This general area of impact has to do with the change in the problem-finding abilities of the managers when using the MDS. The general point to be made here is that the MDS worked very well for pattern recognition, an important part of problem finding. The managers were able to detect trends, see relationships, and generally understand the information they asked for very quickly. This change in problem-finding behavior was obvious from the speed of their reaction as well as their comments. The managers certainly found problems faster with the MDS, and there was some evidence that they found more problems earlier in the decision process.

Much of the information they used was in the form of graphs on the display. These managers had not been in the habit of using graphs, and their initial response to the idea was one of skepticism. However, after the first session they continued to use them and eventually indicated a marked preference for this form of presentation in certain stages of the process.

Problem Solving

The MDS had two major impacts on the problem-solving process of managers. The system portrayed the state of the critical variables which these managers controlled. They changed these variables in the future as they saw fit, and the MDS reflected these changes on the graphs and tables. The graphs of the variables, altered to reflect these new strategies, would in turn suggest other changes, and the managers would follow these new paths, developing strategies that seemed most effective in solving the problem.

The manipulation process by which the managers requested information and computation turned out to be easy for them to use and control. This resulted in their developing several solutions to a problem in an attempt to find one that they felt was "best." In the initial system discussed here, there were no sophisticated algorithms, heuristics, or models to help them to find the "best" solution. However, they did make an attempt, unlike the previous system, to find such a solution. In developing various alternatives they found themselves choosing solutions that had not originally occurred to them. This process of developing several possibilities and selecting among them made them feel that their decisions were better. They felt they were considering more alternatives and looking at more variables, and therefore felt that the quality of their final decision was improving. However, the MDS had no apparent, direct impact on the creative process itself. The creation of an initial solution took place in the minds of the managers. They were responsible for thinking of solutions which they then developed with the aid of the MDS.

The system had a simple exponential forecast routine and there was no basic reason why other models could not be provided. The hardware and time available for this initial project did not allow for this development. More important, the managers did not initially see that any algorithms existed. As the managers used the MDS, they began to see that some decision algorithms were desirable. This is a significant point, since these managers had not been in the habit of developing explicit criteria or structuring the decision variables involved. However, this issue will be discussed in the following chapters.

Communications Role of the MDS

The MDS seems to have fulfilled the role of a communicator. It served as a discipline for stimulating thought and as a medium for communicating ideas between persons. From Chapter 8 and an analysis of the protocol in Appendix D, it is apparent that the MDS is being used to provide two forms of communication. The first form is for the individual himself, and the second involves communication between individuals.

The managers used the device to clarify a point for themselves, or to search for something they did not know. They also used the device for learning. That is, they asked questions of themselves all the way through the process, and in arriving at an answer learned something about the world with which they were dealing. On the other hand, no assertion is being made here that this device was a *good* learning tool. The point is that the managers on occasion would ask themselves a question, develop an answer, and then make some remark to indicate that the answer was not what had been expected. Over time, this resulted in the managers' exhibiting different search behavior as they learned more about the problem with which they were dealing.

The second form of communication was between individuals. This is discussed later in Chapter 8 but seems to have another effect which is less obvious. The managers used the device constantly to make a point to one another. That is, if at some point in the discussion the other sounded doubtful or did not see the issue, it was the MDS that was used to explain the point. As a result of this, the issue was usually clear to all concerned; one could literally point to the problem. One of the managers commented that this was leaving him with a sense of commitment. When asked to expand, his point was as follows:

> If John points out an unusual jump in our plan three months from now and I insist that it is O.K., that we will meet it, then I have a feeling that neither of us is going to forget that I said we could do it. Before [the previous system] the future was so buried that many of the points were not clear and we. . . .

It is too soon to tell if this effect is significant in actual practice. It is interesting, however, that one of the managers should have felt this way. Easy communication led to a clearer understanding of the problem. It may be that the clearer understanding will lead to greater commitment to what have become the joint goals of those involved.

SUMMARY

Nontechnical managers engaged in solving complex problems found that the man/machine combination is a highly convenient, powerful adjunct to their decision process. It provided them with flexible access to a large data-base, but more significantly it allowed them to explore the future. They had the ability to look forward and test strategies easily and simply.

As a result of these features, the decision process changed considerably. Time was reduced sharply, which not only released managerial talent for other problems, but also induced more vigorous, logical, problem solving. The reduction in elapsed time led to management's greater familiarity with the problems' complexities, and, as is discussed in Chapter 8, the reduction in response time led management to explore a wider set of solution strategies.

In addition to the time effect there was a change in the problem-finding and problem-solving processes. Problem finding was characterized by the ease with which a problem could be viewed from various directions. This at least offered the possibility of more effective work in finding relevant problems. Problem solving was enhanced by the access to computational power, the ability to specify the required action easily and simply as it was required, and the resulting creation of several viable solutions.

Communication between the managers was changed considerably with the use of the system. Less effort was required to make one's point clear and less time was spent on discussing misunderstood issues. Communication was simple, and there was some indication that it led to a greater sense of commitment to the fulfillment of the plan that was finally selected.

Chapter 2

THE GENERAL TECHNOLOGY: TERMINAL CHARACTERISTICS

TERMINAL TYPES

THE COMPUTER TERMINAL itself is just another piece of hardware and as such can only be useful to a manager when it is part of a system containing information, computational power, and models. If the system is to be used as support for management decision making, then it must consist of at least the following components:

(1) The manager and his problem area.
(2) The terminal for interface between manager and system.
(3) The software or program to support the manager.
(4) The central computer to drive the terminal.
(5) The data-base that contains information for the problem area.

EXHIBIT 2–1

COMPONENTS OF A MANAGEMENT DECISION SYSTEM

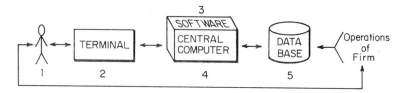

The central computer requirements (item 4) are discussed in Appendix A. Item 2 will be discussed below, and the remainder of the components are discussed in Chapter 6 and Appendix A.

This chapter discusses, in the first section, the characteristics and performance of the two principal types of computer terminals that might be useful for managers. The first of these is the typewriter terminal, and the second the visual-display terminal. The second section of the chapter deals with the advantages and disadvantages of each type of terminal from the standpoint of the manager as a user. It is asserted that the manager and his problems have certain characteristics which tend to make the visual-display terminals much more useful than the typewriter terminals.

Apart from these two types, all other terminals are either special-purpose devices or in the basic research stage. An example of the special-purpose terminals is the IBM data-collection terminal used for production control. This terminal is designed to deal with only a limited set of information. An example of the research terminals is the terminal used for current experiments with voice communication to a computer. At this point in time, there is no indication of any immediately useful results for managerial problem solving from either the research or special-purpose terminals.

Arguments are presented below in support of the assertion that the visual-display, cathode-ray tube (CRT), terminals are presently the most viable alternative for managerial purposes, especially for the manager who is engaged in complex problem solving. Terminals, however, have many uses other than complex problem solving, for example, as simple "windows" into the computer's database for information retrieval (e.g., what is the sales status of red washing machines), and in other fields such as providing a link to computational power to support operations research activity. These other uses will all make some contribution to the effectiveness of those working within the firm, but it may not be necessary for such users to have a graphical CRT device.

Typewriter Terminals

As was mentioned above, terminals fall into two broad categories: typewriter and visual display. The typewriter form of terminal is in almost universal use with interactive computer systems.

It resembles an ordinary electric typewriter and is operated in much the same way. The instructions, commands or data, are typed out in the appropriate format and then transmitted over regular telephone wires to the central computer. There are a few additional special keys, such as "transmit," but basically it is a normal typewriter. The teletype (model 33 and 35) together with the IBM 1050 and 2741 have by far the greatest segment of the market. Some relevant statistics on these devices are given in Exhibit 2–2.

EXHIBIT 2–2

TYPEWRITER TERMINAL STATISTICS

	WPM*	Cost in Dollars per Month (Approx.)	Spaces per Line	Peripherals
Bell 33ASR	100	60	80	KB**; Paper Tape (PT)
" 35ASR	100	125	80	KB; PT
IBM 1050	180	75–150	132	KB; Cards; PT
" 2741	180	75–100	132	KB**

* Words Per Minute.
** Key Board

These devices can accept typed information at a rate faster than any human can generate it—about 14 characters per second. The telephone wires will permit passage of data at 2,400 bits per second or from 75 to 300 characters per second depending on the coding scheme used. Output is constrained by the speed with which the device will type or punch. In general, then, typewriter terminals can be connected via regular telephone lines to the central computer with no loss in performance. Actually, the capacity of the telephone line is so much greater in the case of a typewriter terminal that five terminals can share the same voice-grade line.

Data transmission, while expensive because of present rate structure, is not normally prohibitive on typewriter terminals. These terminals, then, can be placed in any user location that can be reached by telephone line. The line is fast enough to accept all user inputs as fast as they are typed or read in from paper tape. The computer can type responses at a rate of roughly one line every 4 seconds or around 1½ minutes per page. For the newer Inktronic devices that spray ink onto the paper these speeds are less than one second per line and 44 seconds per page.

The user, of course, can run any program, input any data, retrieve information or perform any task for which the software has been written. He can command models, data, programs, or information.

Response time, the computer's answer to a request, is determined by factors such as the type of request, characteristics of the central computer, software system, scheduling rules, number of active users, and so forth. However, with an appropriate computer it can be instantaneous if necessary. The typewriter becomes a direct link between the user and the central computer.

Visual-Display Devices

Visual-display terminals are relative newcomers to the field. The displays that are commercially available as standard equipment have similar functional capabilities. They fall into three general types: (1) alpha-numeric, (2) graphical, and (3) special purpose.

Alpha-Numeric Displays

These are devices which look somewhat like a television set and which are capable of displaying letters, numbers, and in some cases special symbols. They are mostly of the cathode ray tube variety although there are a number of other types. These terminals can be connected by telephone line and are some 20 times faster than typewriter terminals; one page of information can be displayed in four seconds. In addition, these terminals are silent, as there are no mechanical components. Exhibit 2–3 contains a summary of the relevant characteristics of a typical terminal in this class (IBM 2260).

These devices seem to be most useful for structured tasks which do not need graphical output. Simple inquiries for information and routine clerical functions are typical examples. They have had

EXHIBIT 2–3

COMPARISON CHART—VISUAL-DISPLAY TERMINALS

		Computer Displays ARDS	IMLAC PDS–1	IBM 2260	IDI 1009	IBM 2250–1	Adage Agt–30
Purchase Price[1]	High	8,000	20,245	20,325	80,000	95,960	175,000
	Low	7,000	8,900	17,715		72,165	125,000
Screen Size (Inches)[2]		8.25 × 6.4	11.5 × 8	9 × 4	13 × 13	12 × 12	14 × 14
Storage Capacity (Characters)[3]		4,000	4–64K	960	5,120	3,848	16,000
Addressable Points[4]		1081 × 1415	1024 × 1024	Not App.	1024 × 1024	1024 × 1024	128K × 128K
Character Rate Gen. Technique[5]		500 / 7 × 9 Dot	41,600 / 5 × 7 or 7 × 9 Dot	5 × 7 Dot	75,000 / Stroke	67,000 / Stroke	78,000 / Stroke
Max. Data Rate (Char./Sec.)[6]		500	500,000	2,560	Variable	475,000	500,000
Character Rotation[7]		No	No	No	Yes	No	No
Hard Copy[8]		Opt.	Opt.	No	No	No	Opt.
Graphic Input[9]		Opt.	Opt.	No	Yes	Yes	Yes
Vector Capability		Yes	Yes	No	Yes	Yes	Yes

Function Keys[10]	No	No	No	Opt.	Opt.	Yes
Keyboard[11]	58 Key ASC 11	Typewriter	50-Key Typewriter	Opt.	Opt. Typewriter	Teletype
Max. Characters Per Line[12]	80 or 50	72 or 64	80 or 12	130 or 64	74 or 52	112 or 72
Max. Characters Flicker Free[13]	4,000	1,300	960	3,333	2,200	2,600

1 Purchase Price is the manufacturer's list price in quantities of one for a usable range of options.

2 Screen Size is the published viewable screen dimensions.

3 Storage Capacity is the maximum number of characters which may be stored in the terminal for display.

4 Addressable Points describe the number of discrete points which may be used in the horizontal and vertical directions.

5 Character Rate and Generation Technique are the maximum rates at which characters are written on the screen and the method used to generate these characters.

6 Maximum Data Rate is the maximum rate at which characters may be stored at the terminal.

7 Character Rotation is the option which allows characters to be written both vertically and horizontally on the screen.

8 Hard Copy provides a method for connecting a page printer to the terminal for printing textual material.

9 Graphic Input is normally provided with a light-pen, mouse, rand tablet, or similar device. This option provides the user with the ability to point to, or draw, objects on the screen.

10 Function Keys provide a separate keyboard or set of switches to indicate special functions to the computer.

11 Keyboard is the textual input facility.

12 Maximum Characters Per Line describe the largest number of characters in the horizontal direction.

13 Maximum Characters Flicker Free constitute the number of characters which may be displayed before the user can observe flicker from the screen refreshing cycle.

24 *Management Decision Systems*

relatively little actual use outside of military applications compared
with typewriter terminals. Their principal use has been in clerical
tasks where, for example, an order-processing clerk might wish to
examine an order that had been entered directly into the computer
files from some remote location. Another example is an airline
reservations system for linking agents with the central flight information. They also have obvious application in any information
retrieval operation where a remote user needs information from a
central source.

The potential uses for this type of display have scarcely been
touched. The lack of experience due to the few operational on-line
systems, together with what has been the high cost of the displays, have combined to keep the number of users small. Costs
are dropping and, as the economics change, use can be expected
to increase as these alpha-numeric terminals replace typewriter
terminals.

Graphical Display Devices

These visual display devices have full alpha-numeric capability
but, in addition, have the ability to draw vectors and circles, or
any combination of the two. They can be driven by telephone lines
and installed in any convenient location. The graphical capability
is extremely useful as it permits much faster assimilation by the
user of the information content of the display. Patterns and trends,
for example, are easily recognized.

A crucial additional feature of this form of display, if it is to
be used for managerial purposes, is the interactive capability. A
light-pen or some similar device can be pointed at the screen and
the computer system will respond as programmed. With adequate
software this allows the user to specify his requirements to the
system easily and rapidly without typing.

These devices have been even less used and less available than
the alpha-numeric category. Their cost is higher, their requirements
for sophisticated software are higher, and the demands on the
user's system design quite stringent. On-line data-base availability
can be a limiting factor for many years. These devices are discussed in more detail in Appendix A, as these display devices have
by far the greatest potential for management use.

Terminal Characteristics

From the above discussion it is clear that terminals of each type have certain obvious characteristics which make them potentially useful to management. These characteristics are summarized below and are discussed later in the context of the particular experimental setting. However, part of this usefulness is entirely dependent on the development of some form of multiple-access computer which provides the managers economically with a common data-base and significant computing power. Similarly, provision of adequate software to support the manager is also a necessary feature. These two issues are discussed in some depth in Appendix A.

From the research in this and other experiments[1] some simple conclusions can be drawn about the relevant characteristics of each form of terminal from a management standpoint. These are discussed below in summary form, as they are only assertions until further experimental evidence has been collected.

Interactive Computer Terminals

There are a few attributes of terminal systems in general that distinguish this form of computer power from the traditional batch processing. These are:

(1) *Convenience.* The user has access to the terminal in the privacy of his own office, or at some location of his choice, at times when he is ready to use it.
(2) *Interaction.* The user interacts with the computer systems and can modify his requests for information in light of his progress toward his immediate goal. This flexibility allows him to receive only the information he requires, thus avoiding the process of sifting through voluminous general purpose reports for the information he needs.
(3) *Direct Contact.* The user is not forced through any process of explanation to some intermediary who then deals with the computer. He, or his own staff, can specify his information needs directly.

---

[1] See (49).

(4) *Response Time.* The user receives an answer to his problem or inquiry very much faster than in any other way; typically, this response can be measured in seconds.

Typewriter Terminals

Typewriter terminals, as opposed to visual-display terminals have three unique characteristics which determine their applicability in any given situation:

(1) *Cost.* This form of terminal is inexpensive ($40–$150 per month) and widely available which makes it easy to install as part of a management information system.
(2) *Hard Copy.* As a direct result of the communication media, the user has a copy of his "answers" right in front of him.
(3) *Typewriter Aspects.* This form of terminal does suffer from all of the disadvantages of typewriters. They tend to be fairly noisy, are limited in speed by their mechanical components, and require the user to be able to type.

Alpha-Numeric Visual-Display Terminals

These terminals use a screen on which to display the information, and are limited to letters and numbers.

(1) *Hard Copy.* This has to be an added feature. Most of those marketed today do not have the ability to provide paper printouts directly. Those few that do are considerably more expensive. There are a variety of ways around this however. An example might be to have a teletype available or a Polaroid camera.
(2) *Speed.* These terminals are much faster and quieter than the typewriter terminals, a factor of 20 being typical for speed by comparison with typewriter terminals.
(3) *Cost.* The cost, at the moment, is higher (Exhibit 2–3). This has to be balanced against the speed and silence. A typewriter terminal can produce a line of text in 4 seconds and a 20-line page in 1½ minutes. The corresponding figures for a typical alpha-numeric terminal are 4 lines per second or a page in 5 seconds.

Graphical Visual Display Terminals

These terminals have all of the characteristics noted above. In addition, they have two very important features:

(1) Vector drawing capability is a feature of considerable power in a management terminal. Graphical portrayal of data seems to be easier for the human mind to comprehend[2] and can frequently be used to condense large amounts of data. This connection between graphical representation and comprehension by the manager is not yet fully supported by research evidence, but it does fit in with our experience and was a point mentioned by all of those participating in this experiment.

(2) In addition to the vector capability is the variety of modes of interaction offered by these terminal systems. There is the keyboard, similar to that of the typewriter terminal, but in addition there are the light-pen and function-keys. Both of these last two items offer simple, flexible interaction which is not too complicated for an intelligent, yet ignorant, user. With the visual-display terminals the screen is "alive" and the computer with its associated software can recognize what is being pointed at with the light-pen and respond accordingly. This permits simple interaction, which with good software can be very powerful.

GENERAL CONCLUSIONS

These general characteristics of a graphical terminal provide a tool which is simple to use yet powerful in its response. If designed appropriately, such terminals can be very effective in a management setting. A suggested set of such design characteristics is given in Appendix A, together with an explanation of the major components of a visual display. It is worth noting at this point that *no major* manufacturer currently offers, in its regular line, a graphical terminal that has all the features discussed in Appendix A as being desirable for managerial use. One typical terminal, for

---

[2] See (8), (78).

example, has room for only 75 characters across the screen, which is not enough for many managerial situations, nor can it be connected directly to phone lines. Fortunately there are small manufacturers (see Exhibit 2–3) that do offer appropriate terminals and these can be connected to most multiple-access computers.

Chapter 3

PROBLEM CHARACTERISTICS FOR THE MANAGEMENT DECISION SYSTEM

THE MDS WILL BE MORE EFFECTIVE when used on certain classes of problems than it will be when used on others. This system is certainly no panacea for all management problems. It has some strengths which are appropriate as support for managers in certain decision-making situations, and these are discussed briefly here.

This project was primarily concerned with the impact and potential of management decision systems and not with developing the complete dimensions of the spectrum of problems on which such systems can be used. However, it is important to identify the characteristics of the management problem used in this experiment as it then becomes possible to say that any problem having such characteristics is likely to be affected by the MDS in much the same way. The characteristics involved with this problem would seem to be typical of many of the ill-defined, difficult problems with which managers have to deal. This suggests that this experiment can be generalized to meet many of the important problems with which responsible managers are faced.

The characteristics identified below can be found in both line and staff problems at all levels of management and in all functional areas. For example, many aspects of budgeting, profit planning, production planning, advertising strategy selection, and formal long-range planning have these characteristics.

There are a number of fairly clear characteristics of the problem with which the managers were concerned in this study. The most fundamental of these, as has already been discussed, is that the problem is "unprogrammed." That is, it is an ill-structured, poorly defined problem area. Indeed, much of the difficulty the managers experience comes from "finding" the relevant problem in the first place. Such problems cannot be solved by a series of fixed decision rules. They are, to use Simon's terminology, not amenable to algorithmic forms of solution. This point is discussed in Chapter 5 and will not be pursued further here.

IDENTIFIABLE PROBLEM CHARACTERISTICS

The remainder of the problem characteristics are less well documented and have been obtained from close examination of the particular problem and its bottlenecks as discussed below. The identifiable characteristics attributable to this problem are:

(1) Large data-base.
(2) High requirements for data manipulation.
(3) Managerial judgment required.
(4) Complex interrelationships.
(5) Multidimensionality.
(6) Different functional groups involved.
(7) Economic significance, high payoff from good solutions.
(8) Dynamic environment.

These are discussed below, but the general point being made is that if any other management problem exhibits these characteristics, then the impact of the MDS is likely to be similar to the experience in this project. Of course, these eight dimensions can individually be quite different from project to project and yet the problem area could usefully use an MDS. For example, one problem could have a small data-base (1), and require a large amount of manipulation (2), while another problem might have a very large data-base and trivial computation. Both problems might justify the use of an MDS.

Looking at these problem characteristics in greater detail:

Large Data-Base

A Management Decision System is useful when the data-base is of sufficient size that it cannot be maintained or searched manually within any reasonable time span. Reasonable, in this instance, implies that the search activity does not interfere with the decision-making process. The precise sizes and timing involved will always be dependent on the specific situation. In this instance the data-base for any one decision cycle was on the order of 73,000 elements (individual numbers) and as suggested in Chapter 4 this was a large enough volume to interfere with the decision process.

High Requirements for Data Manipulation

If the overall problem-solving process involves a large amount of computation or data manipulation, then convenient computational power is desirable. This might occur either with a large data-base and relatively little manipulation or with a smaller data-base and high amounts of computation. In this instance (see Appendix D), a typical strategy under the old process might involve recalculating 800 numbers; this was done approximately 20 times in the course of a typical month's decision process. With the new system this was 10 to 20 times higher.

Managerial Judgment Required

The problem is also characterized by a considerable degree of judgment. There is judgment required both to determine what constitutes the problem as well as judgment involved in generating and selecting answers. In other words both the "problem-finding" and "problem-solution" processes require managerial judgment. The decision maker does not have good algorithms or decision rules that allow him to arrive at *the* answer. Instead he is forced to apply his judgment and intuition to the problem and arrive at some acceptable solution.

This characteristic can also be thought of in the following terms. Since the problem is unprogrammed there are unlikely to be many criteria that hold for all situations. Hence, no algorithm can readily detect trends or pick out situations that call for closer attention. The human being can do this readily and quickly by drawing on his "experience" and deciding in an intuitive, judgmental way whether or not a given situation requires further attention.

Complex Interrelationships

The effects of a possible solution in this problem-solving process are hard to predict because of the size of the data-base on which the solution has an impact. Similarly, prediction can be difficult because of the complex interrelationships among the variables. In either case this can cause considerable inconvenience by substantially increasing both the time and the cost of arriving at the impact of a potential solution. This characteristic also makes it difficult for the problem solver to detect the cause and effect relationships among the variables. When these interrelationships pass some threshold level, a manager's intuition ceases to be adequate and the MDS becomes an appropriate means of support.

Multidimensionality

The problem has several dimensions along which one can measure performance and the relevant one is not always known in advance. In general, one can assert that the complete list of dimensions may not be known and that, certainly, the relevant one at any given moment in time will not be known ahead of time. For example, adequate protection from stockouts of inventory may be more important in some months than dollars of profit. This in turn may not hold for certain models and might also be different if there is the possibility of a strike at the manufacturing facility. When there are several dimensions, particularly with trade-offs among them, it can be useful to have the power of the MDS.

Different Functional Groups Involved

This problem has several persons involved at different stages. Each person has some particular skill or information that is relevant to the decision-making process and this must be combined with information from the specialists from the other functional areas before a final decision can be reached. Therefore, this process involves not only an individual solving part of the problem himself, but also group review and problem solving. This then involves a communication function where people with one particular set of attitudes have to provide and receive information from another group, who in turn have their own view of the world. In such situations a powerful communications medium, such as the MDS, can be a useful part of the decision process.

Economic Significance

The costs involved in developing and running an MDS have to be more than offset by the benefits derived from the system. Initially such a system should be used where the payoff from making a good decision is high. Decisions with large resource implications can show significant dollar gains with improved decision making. Initial problems on which an MDS is to be used should have high economic payoff—they should be "key" decisions for the organization or manager.

Dynamic Environment

Problems that are in a setting where the environment is changing rapidly can be significantly affected by an MDS. Managers have a wide range of activities and cannot stay on top of a constantly changing situation. Adaptive models, good filters, flexible access to the data-base and other attributes of an MDS offer the manager real help in detecting shifting patterns in the key variables. In addition, of course, there are the benefits that accrue in formalizing the information flow and freeing up the manager's time to look for new relevant variables.

The above list of problem characteristics follows rather directly from an analysis of the former problem-solving process. These characteristics are stated in general terms and it is suggested that they are, in fact, typical of most significant, "unprogrammed," business problems. We would assert that any decision-making process involving a problem that has some mixture of the above eight characteristics is likely to be affected by the Management Decision System in much the same way as the one observed here.

FRAMEWORK FOR DECISION MAKING

Since problems of this type are large and somewhat messy it becomes necessary to impose some structure. To understand the decision process and to observe changes in its content require an explicit model of the activity involved.

What is needed is a framework of the decision-making process in which the impact of the Management Decision System (MDS) can be examined. In the following chapters both the old and new decision processes are cast in terms of the framework discussed in this chapter. It is suggested that the characteristics of the framework, described below, are viable at any level in the organization and in any function. Therefore, whatever impact is experienced in this particular experimental situation on these characteristics is likely to hold true in other similar decision-making situations. The process and results of the MDS, then, will be monitored to determine if the areas of hypothesized impact are correct, and if so how these findings will apply to other situations. The results will provide an idea as to the uses and likely impact of a remote access visual display terminal system (MDS) on the management decision-making process.

With terminal systems, as in any management system, it is important to be able to understand the costs and benefits involved. The cost side is fairly straightforward and is discussed briefly in Chapter 6. The benefit side is more difficult to evaluate but equally essential. The framework discussed in this chapter facilitates one form of cost/benefit study. In order to arrive at a notion of the benefits to be derived from the system, one has to be able to compare performance before and after the introduction of the new system. Comparison implies a measurement process and this obviously requires some framework or yardstick.

The approach taken to this problem[1] in the study is to propose a model of the decision-making process. The former process is then analyzed in this framework. Following the introduction of the new system, the process that develops with it is subjected to the same analysis, and a comparison is made between them. This then

---

[1] See (48) for elaboration of this issue.

allows one to identify differences between the various subparts of the process. These differences can then be separated into those for which a dollar value can be attached and those which must remain qualitative. These qualitative differences can be examined by the managers concerned and matched with the costs involved. They then are forced to make their own evaluation as to whether these system benefits are worth the cost. This puts the decision, and the information available, on those best able to make it: the managers directly concerned.

The literature on decision making did not provide any complete ready-made framework to use as a convenient medium for this research. Therefore, such a framework had to be developed. The material discussed below is an extension of Simon's[2] work on the nature of problem solving.

The problem was basically one of building a framework that would portray the decision-making process with somewhat greater discrimination than Simon's "Intelligence, Design, Choice" stages. Following the literature discussion such a framework is developed and presented in sufficient detail to allow it to be used in measuring the impact of the Management Decision System (MDS) on management problem solving.

The proposed framework is shown diagrammatically in Exhibit 3–1 and discussed in the remainder of the chapter. In summary, however, the decision-making process can be thought of as being divided into three major phases: (1) Intelligence, or the search for problems; (2) Design, or the invention of solutions; and (3) Choice, or the selection of a course of action. Each of these major phases has three subphases: (a) Generation of input data; (b) Manipulation of the data; and (c) Selection for the following phase. This framework applies equally to programmed decisions (those that are well-structured) and nonprogrammed decisions (decisions that are ill-structured).

---

[2] See (70).

EXHIBIT 3–1

FRAMEWORK FOR THE DECISION-MAKING PROCESS

		Intelligence	Design	Choice
S T R U C T U R E D	Generation			
	Manipulation			
	Selection			
U N S T R U C T U R E D	Generation	1 Low*	4 Medium	7 High
	Manipulation	2 High	5 High	8 Low
	Selection	3 High	6 High	9 Low

* Expected impact of the Management Decision System.

MAJOR PHASES OF DECISION MAKING

Decision making can usefully be divided into several substeps. In the particular framework developed for use in this research, the intelligence activity refers to the process that the decision maker goes through in endeavoring to identify problems, or potential problems, within the area for which he is responsible. The design activity refers to the efforts of the decision maker, once he has identified the problem, to create a solution to it. This creation process *ideally* involves testing the solution in order to arrive at a good estimate of its impact. The choice activity is concerned with selecting a solution, or course of action, from among those created in the design phase. This can be thought of as matching the expected impacts of the various solutions against some model of the desired results. These three major phases are part of every decision-making process, but they are at too macro a level to be of immediate assistance in the present problem.

The proposed framework, therefore, has three additional subphases, applicable to each of the major phases. There do not seem to be any experimental facts on decision making that bear directly on this problem, so one is left with common experience and a close examination of the present methods used by the managers in question.

LITERATURE ON DECISION MAKING

In an early article[3] Simon pointed out the severe limitations of the economist's classical theory of decision making. This three-step classical process he asserted was as follows:

(1) An individual is presented with a number of different, specified, alternative courses of action;

(2) To each of these alternatives is attached a set of consequences that will ensue if that alternative is chosen;

(3) The individual has a system of preferences or "utilities" that permit him to rank all sets of consequences according to preference and to choose that alternative that has the preferred consequences. In the case of business decisions the criterion for ranking is generally assumed to be profit.

Simon went on to point out that this is an inadequate representation of the decision-making process and that four other elements needed to be added. These elements were:

---

[3] See (74), page 237.

(1) The alternatives are not usually "given" but must be sought, and hence it is necessary to include the search for alternatives as an important part of the process.

(2) The information as to what consequences are attached to which alternatives is seldom a "given," but instead the search for consequences is another important segment of the decision-making task.

(3) The comparisons among alternatives are not usually made in terms of a simple, single criterion like profit. One reason is that there are often important consequences that are so intangible as to make an evaluation in terms of profit difficult or impossible. In place of searching for the "best" alternative, the decision maker is usually concerned with finding a satisfactory alternative—one that will attain a specified goal and at the same time satisfy a number of auxiliary conditions.

(4) Often, in the real world, the problem itself is not a "given" but instead, searching for significant problems to which organizational attention should be turned, becomes an important significant task.[4]

With the addition of these four points, Simon showed that a business decision that he monitored matched this framework. Elsewhere Simon generalized from this example and asserted that the decision-making process falls into three phases. These are discussed at length in *Organizations*,[5] Chapters 6 and 7, and are summarized by Simon in *The New Science of Management Decision*[6] as follows:

> The first phase of the decision-making process—searching the environment for conditions calling for decisions—I shall call "Intelligence" activity (borrowing the military meaning of intelligence). The second phase—inventing, developing, and analyzing possible courses of action—I shall call design activity. The third phase—selecting a particular course of action from those available —I shall call choice activity.

Thus the essence of this part of Simon's work is the claim that the process of making a decision, any decision in any part of a busi-

[4] *Ibid.*, p. 238.
[5] See Simon (42).
[6] See Simon (72).

ness, can be broken up into three phases: Intelligence, Design, Choice. These three segments hold true no matter what the specific problem may be.

Other authors such as Gore,[7] Jones,[8] Barnard,[9] Polya,[10] and Kepner,[11] have discussed the problem-solving process in terms compatible with Simon's. In each case, however, their objectives were different from those with which we are concerned. For the purposes of this study it is necessary to have a level of detail one level greater in order to discriminate among the various segments of the decision-making process. Analysis of the former problem-solving process (see Chapter 5) suggested the further breakdown into subphases. These subphases are:

(a) *Generation* of input data for the manipulation subphase.
(b) *Manipulation* of the data to arrive at some appropriate input for the selection subphase.
(c) *Selection* of some output to go to the next phase of the process or to be implemented as a decision.

With the addition of these subphases we have the nine-celled framework in the upper half of Exhibit 3-1. However, there is a further important distinction between structured and unstructured types of decisions.[12]

The most succinct statement of this probably occurs in Simon's *The New Science of Management Decision,* where he identifies the ends of the decision-making continuum as programmed and nonprogrammed decisions. "Decisions are nonprogrammed to the extent they are novel, unstructured and consequential. There is no cut and dried method for handling the problem. . . ."[13] Pro-

---

[7] See W. S. Gore, *Administration Decision Making: A Heuristic Model.* John Wiley & Sons, Inc., 1964, pp. 49–112.

[8] See M. H. Jones, *Executive Decision Making.* Richard D. Irwin, Inc., 1957.

[9] See Barnard (4).

[10] See Polya (54).

[11] See Tregoe and Kepner (80).

[12] Simon (72), p. 5.

[13] *Ibid.,* p. 6.

grammed decisions are the opposite, well-structured with fixed routines for handling them.

Dividing the framework into the two types of decisions (Exhibit 3–1) then provides 18 cells which, it is asserted, provide one reasonable and useful description of the management decision-making process. No claim is being made that this framework is better than any other that could be developed. The important issue is that there should be *some* framework to help in the analysis of unstructured problem solving. The particular choice is probably a matter of personal preference and the use to which it is being put.

The problem being investigated here is an unstructured kind of problem which means that only the bottom half of the framework is involved. Structured problems, almost by definition, are of less interest as it is obvious that terminal systems, visual or otherwise, *can* be used in solving such problems. Whether such systems *will* be used to make decisions in the structured area is largely a matter of cost and the preferences of those involved.

This chapter has laid out a simple framework in which to look at the decision-making process. It is asserted that this framework usefully describes the steps necessary in all decision-making situations. Certainly in the environment discussed in the following chapter it seems to provide a close and consistent model of what actually took place.

Chapter 4

FORMER DECISION-MAKING PROCESS

IT SEEMS APPROPRIATE AT THIS STAGE to provide an understanding of the problem and the problem environment in which the MDS was used. The description is not intended as a detailed mirror image of the actual situation, but enough information is given so that a clear picture of the task facing the managers can be seen. The first section discusses the environment the managers work in, both in the company as a whole and in the specific division. This description covers the organization structure as it was at the time of the initial experiment; since then there have been a number of changes. The second section is concerned with a description of the problem itself, and the final section with the decision-making process by which the managers originally solved the problem.

ENVIRONMENT

The company involved is a large multiproduct firm with sales in the billions of dollars. The company is decentralized by product group with some 70 divisions producing everything from large turbines to electric toothbrushes. The marketing organization (see organization chart, Exhibit 4–1) for the consumer product groups is a separate division and is responsible on both a dollar profit and volume basis for its performance in selling the various products.

EXHIBIT 4–1

Organization Chart—Consumer Group

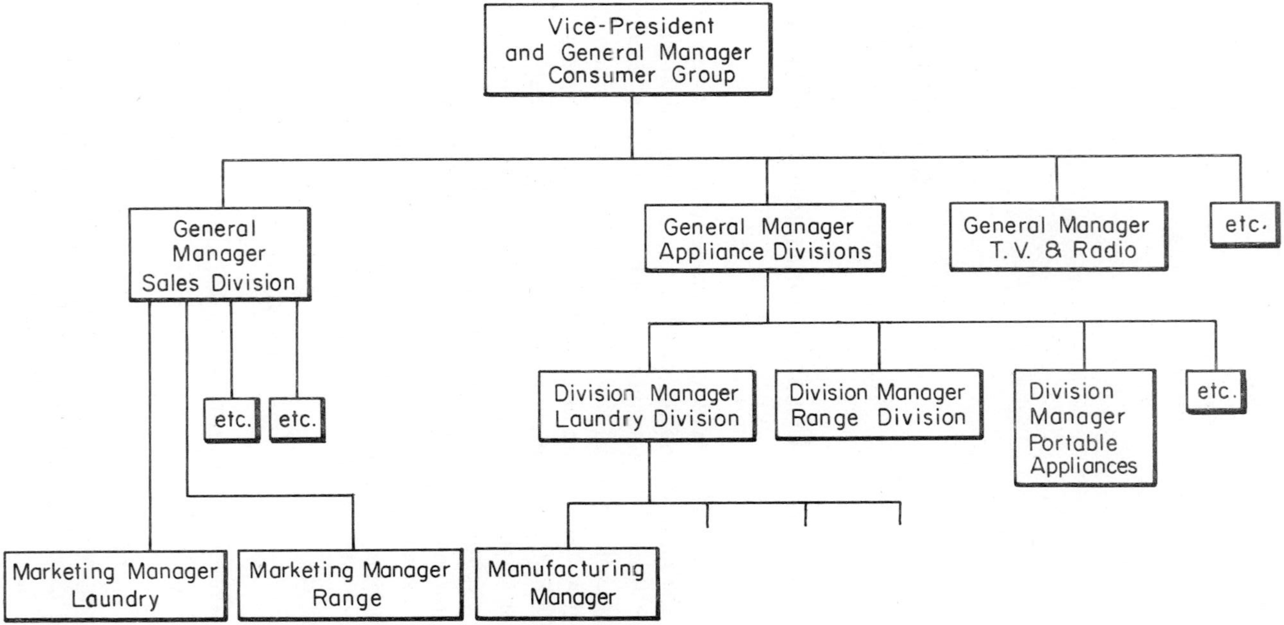

This division buys from a number of different factories that produce the various consumer products and also operates and maintains its own warehousing facilities. The "purchase" price is a transfer price arrived at in a traditional[1] fashion.

The company as a whole has been a pioneer with real-time order entry systems and maintains a central computer facility as a central data bank and switching center. The activities of this center and the other computer installations within the company have led to a certain amount of familiarity with computers and related technology among the division's personnel. At the time of this experiment the division had a "standard" form of organization structure (Exhibit 4–2) which had operated successfully for a number of years. This organization assigned certain specific products, or groups of products, to the marketing managers, who then performed their functions in relation to that product grouping.

The positions with which we are particularly concerned are those of the managers who were responsible for a particular task: the market planning manager, the production manager, and the marketing manager. Their task is discussed below.

TASK DESCRIPTION

General

The decision-making process that these managers were concerned with is a complex planning problem. They had to derive a plan for the allocation of resources in both the production and the marketing areas. Every month they developed both a production plan and a sales plan for the following twelve months. On the basis of these plans, the manufacturing personnel made their specific decisions about work force levels, production scheduling, and so forth. Similarly, the marketing people considered the specifics of such things as pricing and merchandising strategy. The production and marketing plans that these managers devised formed the goal for all the operational people during the coming months. In short, they were concerned with setting goals for the production and marketing divisions.

---

[1] See Dearden (21).

EXHIBIT 4-2

ORGANIZATION CHART—DIVISION LEVEL

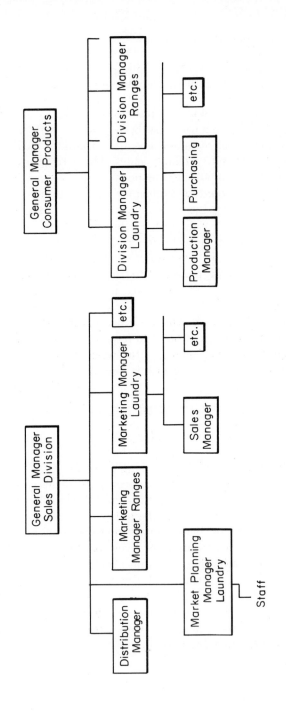

The marketing side started from a computer-based sales forecast. This was modified by the marketing manager's judgment to reflect what he saw as a reasonable objective during the coming months. In essence, he started with a sales forecast and ended with a marketing plan. Similarly, the production plan started as a forecast of requirements to meet the initial forecast of sales. The production forecast was then modified to reflect changes in the marketing plan and also modified to reflect manufacturing's goals of efficient production. It was then used as the specific goal for the coming months and formed the basis for all detailed production planning and scheduling.

Specific Problem

The problem the market planning manager had was one of setting specific production targets for the various products for which he was responsible. He was pressured (see Exhibit 4–3) on the one side by the sales people who wanted to have ample supplies of all products everywhere, and on the other side by the production divisions who were responsible for inventories and wished to keep these as low as possible as well as minimize their production costs. The market planning manager (MPM), then, sat between these two parties and attempted to make a decision that was best for the company as a whole. To do this he had to balance the expected demand, in light of the merchandising plans, against the inventory available and the production already scheduled or in process. Thus, he had to evaluate the following major elements:

(1) Expected demand
(2) Merchandising plans
(3) Available inventory
(4) Production availability

Expected Demand

Of these four items the expected demand was clearly the most difficult to assess. There has been a notable lack of success in developing "good" forecasting algorithms that can be used directly

EXHIBIT 4–3

FACTORS AFFECTING THE DECISION-MAKING PROCESS

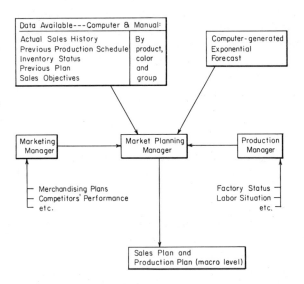

in such situations. It also seems fairly clear that, in fact, there will never be success using traditional algorithmic methods because the phenomenon being predicted is a highly complex one which has a multitude of interacting variables, the relative strength of these changing with time.

Expected demand in this instance was not only a measure of the latent potential in the market place. It was also a figure of actual sales expected. This figure depended, rather obviously, on factors (2), (3), and (4) to a large extent. For example, if the salesmen were encouraged to sell a particular model (merchandising plans), then this markedly affected demand, while the available inventory and production affected sales. (If the product was not in the right place at the right time, there might not be any sale.)

The forecasting of basic (latent) demand is a difficult process, and the forecasting of actual sales is even more difficult. No algorithms can deal with both of these problems; what has been done is to use the best algorithm available for the basic demand portion and modify it for forecasting, using managerial judgment to take account of the impact of merchandising plans, inventory availability, and production capacity. After much experimentation, those involved determined that a variation on an exponential smoothing model gave them the "best" estimate of basic demand.

The exponential forecasting model basically followed the standard format. It had a trend for the product group as a whole, as well as seasonal factors. The model was run on a batch computer, geographically distant from the headquarters management group. The results of the run were forwarded to the managers involved. It was not at all practical under the original system, or most batch systems, for the manager to suggest or test out changes to the basic model in the course of arriving at an answer to his specific problem in any given month.

Merchandising Plans

The determination of what the merchandising plans would be lay entirely within the marketing manager's (MM) discretion. He decided what he should do in this area in order to meet his sales and profit targets established at the beginning of the year. The realization of his merchandising plans obviously depended in part upon the availability of production.

The problem for the market planning manager was to translate the marketing manager's plans into a concrete number of units sold. Thus a heavy advertising campaign for a particular model in the Midwest had to be translated into a model-by-model expected sales figure if the MPM was to plan for the overall demand.

Available Inventory

This component of the problem was very straightforward as it simply involved a listing of the current inventory in all warehouses and in the pipeline. This was available to the market planning manager as a computer print-out, broken down by model. The currency and accuracy of this report were satisfactory in all respects for this decision. The problem that arose was simply one of sheer volume—the report was 2 to 3 inches thick and contained the status of all models and styles in all locations. Finding any specific model was time-consuming and combining models in some fashion other than the one provided was difficult. That is, if the listing was arranged by specific models within regions, and the manager wanted to know how many luxury models were colored yellow, this became a time-consuming process.

Production Availability

In both the overcapacity and undercapacity situation the production process placed some real constraints on the marketing manager's plans. This was true not only from his own divisional point of view but also from the total corporation standpoint, that is, maximization of profits within the present structure of market and company.

In either an undercapacity or overcapacity situation at the factory, the model mix designed to minimize production costs and inventory was unlikely to be what the marketing manager would like, and equally unlikely to match actual demand in any given period.

In an overcapacity situation there was the further complication of having to choose which products to produce and which not to produce, in the event that all could be sold. Trade-offs here could not simply be on the basis of current profit since customer good will, promised delivery dates, and so forth, all were a necessary part in the decision.

The market planning manager, therefore, had to have some means by which to arrive at these trade-offs. In this instance he received from the production personnel, based on their estimates of demand, a preliminary production schedule for the time period involved. This had to be reconciled with the marketing manager's plans. This reconciliation comprised one of the largest problems of the market planning manager's job.

As is explained in the next section, the original method of arriving at production figures was based on an exponential forecast of demand, modified initially as the MPM saw fit, to arrive at a figure for expected sales by model—sales figures that were realizable from a production standpoint. The problem of setting production levels, then, was not one of simply sales forecasting; the realities of efficient production, inventory levels, and merchandising plans all had to be considered. In addition, the figures finally produced had a certain psychological function to perform. They were set at a level which the MPM believed would actually result in delivery of the number of units he wanted to the field. This requested level might be a different number from that which he actually expected to sell.

This number was arrived at by the process described in the remainder of this chapter and in Chapter 5. In general, though, the process was one of negotiation based on each participant's view of the actual situation and his division's goals.

PROCESS DESCRIPTION

The process used by the managers to solve the problem was one that had evolved over time and was still, very properly, in a state of change. The *basic* process, however, had remained fairly stable over the past few years.

Technology in this period had not changed significantly although more information had become available from computer-based files and hence was more up to date. The process was characterized by segmentation which was forced onto the manager by the length of time necessary to compile and manipulate data. This resulted (see flow chart, Exhibit 4–4) in quite distinct phases which added to the elapsed time necessary to complete the job as well as contributing to a distinct lack of continuity in the task of solving the problem.

In summary, the flow chart describes a process where the market planning manager started with a computer-generated forecast and modified this to reflect what he felt was really possible in the way of sales. These figures, for aggregates (i.e., tumblers, agitators, washers), were then discussed jointly in several working sessions with the marketing manager until agreement was reached. The entire process was repeated at the detailed model level. When the models were completed there was normally some discrepancy between, for example, the sum of all the tumbler models and the

EXHIBIT 4–4

FLOW CHART OF THE FORMER DECISION-MAKING PROCESS

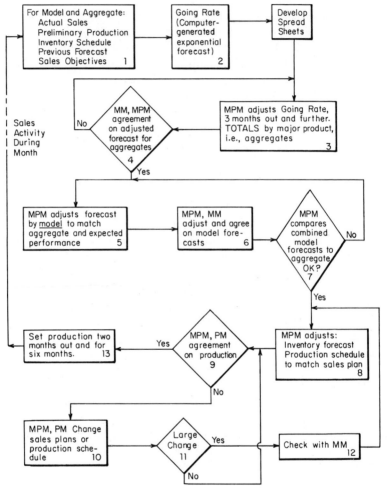

figures developed for tumblers as an aggregate. These were then resolved. A somewhat similar series of discussions then took place with production planning and manufacturing personnel to arrive at a feasible production plan that would meet the sales department's plans.

From Exhibit 4–4 it can be seen that the MPM started with the computer and manual data discussed previously. From this, he and his staff developed spread sheets (Exhibit 4–5) with the data drawn from the various different sources and laid out together. The MPM (3)[2] then used the historical data on the form (Exhibit 4–5), plus his informal knowledge of special events, and modified the exponential forecast to reflect what he felt would happen. The MPM (4) then met with the MM to discuss this forecast. They negotiated any differences and finally agreed on an aggregate figure. This process was then repeated at the model level (5, 6). The staff were heavily involved as there was considerable clerical work involved in developing the spread sheets. When the MPM and MM had reached agreement on the model level, the combined totals of these had to be reconciled with the initial aggregate forecast (7). When this was complete and detailed production and inventory implications laid out (8) there was a series of meetings with the production people.

The MPM negotiated changes in the proposed production schedule with the production people to match their constraints

EXHIBIT 4–5

Sample Spread Sheet (Partial Only)*

TUMBLER	JAN	FEB	MAR	APR	MAY	JUN	JUL	- Total (12mos.)
1967 Actual	1635	2004	2654	2150	2400	2600		
1968 Actual	1820	2430	2300					
Going Rate				2100	2200	2400	2400	
Previous Fcst			2800	2300	2600	2600		
Current Fcst				2200	2300	2600		
1968 Objectives	1700	2100	2500	2700	2600	2700		
Production:								
Actual		2000	1500					
Planned				2500	2000	2200		
Inventory-Factory	1000	800	900	1200	1500	1000		
Total	3000	2600	1800	2200	2000	1800		
Objective	4000	4100	4200	4200	4400	4800	4800	

* Spread sheet developed early April. Sample only, data are illustrative.

---

[2] Number in parentheses indicates box number in Exhibit 4–4.

more closely (9, 10). As changes were made they in turn often affected the sales strategy and so had to be checked with the sales group (11, 12).

Exhibit 4–6 contains a time-phased chart of how this process took place in a typical month. The elapsed time was some 20 working days of which approximately 6 were spent in meetings. The elapsed time was long for two major reasons. There was a great deal of clerical work involved in pulling the information together on the spread sheets. As a change was suggested, it required re-working all the spread sheets to generate the new numbers. To do this work required from two to ten hours, depending on the task. The second reason for the longer elapsed time was the simple logistical problem of arranging a time when three busy managers were all free to attend.

Appendix D contains a skeleton description of the former decision-making process and provides an overview of the steps described in Exhibit 4–4. Appendix D also contains a detailed description of the process, including actual protocols where they seemed appropriate. This description provides more information on the kinds of decisions and the characteristics of the process.

From Appendix D it is clear that the process was largely intuitive, there were few rules, and the managers concerned had no explicit system for considering problems or arriving at solutions. That is, the identification of a problem was intuitive as was the design of a strategy for solution and the evaluation of the impact of the strategy chosen.

Similarly the process was characterized by a large amount of negotiation. There were few facts to base strategies on, so the participants bargained on the basis of the way they felt a proposed solution might affect the plan. Bargaining, based on individual expectations, does not always lead to very effective planning.

The linear planning sequence, with interruptions between sessions, led to some loss in continuity. Arguments raised vociferously in one session were not even mentioned in the next. The protocol indicates the surprise of the managers on some occasions when the data revealed a certain status of their products, but does not seem to reveal any formal learning or the development of consistent criteria on their part.

EXHIBIT 4-6

TIME SPECTRUM—FORMER PROCESS

Days	1	2	3	4	5	6	7	8	9	10	11	12	13	14	15	16	17	18	19	20
Maintain and Transcribe	X	X	X	X																
Exponential Forecast					X															
Develop Initial Current Forecast					X	X	X													
Meet on Total Forecast							X	X												
Adjust Total Forecast									X											
Develop Detail Forecast							X	X	X	X										
Meet on Detail Forecast										X										
Adjust Detail Forecast											X	X								
Agree on Detail Forecast											X	X	X	X						
Generate Tentative Production Schedule														X	X					
Meet with Factory—Agree on Problem Areas														X	X	X				
Change Forecast—Develop Tentative Solutions																X	X			
Meet with Factory—Discuss Solutions																	X	X		
Develop Final Production Schedule																		X	X	X

In summary, the protocol reveals the former process to have
been one that used computer-generated data as input to a sequential decision process. This process involved two specialists and an
arbitrator and was an informal, unstructured series of sessions
which resulted in a resource allocation plan for the balance of a
twelve-month year.

BOTTLENECKS IN THE FORMER PROCESS

If this former process is analyzed in terms of the framework
discussed in Chapter 3, it then turns out to have a series of bottlenecks, each of which hinders the managers in their search for a
solution. For example, in the first step of the process, when the
managers were looking for the major problems, they had considerable difficulty in identifying and agreeing on the major problems to be found from the large data-base. Situations where they
were already in trouble were clear enough, but finding potential
problems was difficult, and was made more so by the volume of
data involved. In Exhibit 4–7 this has been listed in Cell 1 (Intel-
ligence/Generation) as the primary problem at that stage in the
process. The discussion below is designed to provide a flavor of the
kinds of problems the managers had in solving their problem
under the old system. These problems have been grouped in clus-
ters in the general framework that is being used for analysis. Each
of the points in Exhibit 4–7 is discussed below.

Large Data-Base

The size of the data-base was the most limiting factor in this
cell as there were a large number of data elements. The former
data-base, although in machine sensible form, was only available
at fixed periods, and in a fixed format. This involved large quantities of printed paper which had then to be dealt with manually.
About 8,000 numbers from the data-base of 75,000 elements were
transcribed every month onto 25 spread sheets. These numbers
came from three different sources each involving a different computer print-out.

EXHIBIT 4–7

Bottlenecks in the Previous Decision-Making Process

	Intelligence	Design	Choice
Generation	1. (a) Large data-base	4. (a) Implementation of a strategy (b) Conceptualization of strategy	7. (a) Solution space not explored
Manipulation	2. (a) Large quantity of computation (b) Low information content (c) Variable operations required	5. (a) Large quantity of computation (b) Variable operations required	8. (a) Multiple criteria for comparing solutions
Selection	3. (a) Different criteria over time (b) Time requirements (c) Cognitive limitations	6. (a) Implications of the solution on other variables	9. (a) Comparison of multidimensional alternatives

Large Quantity of Computation

The size of the data-base resulted in a considerable amount of manipulation, so much in fact that only the simplest and easiest forms of manipulation were used, those of transcribing the key elements, and simple arithmetic, as discussed in Appendix D. Approximately 16,000 numbers were recalculated manually in each monthly process.

Low Information Content

Not only was the data-base large, but the clues that indicated potential problems were not known in advance. That is, neither the variables nor the magnitude of the deviations were known before the problem-solving process began. This was due to the fact that they were a function of the current state of the system and the expected future performance. Thus, it was *not* possible to make a prior list and use it in some mechanized form.

The process of gaining familiarity with the data, in order to comprehend fully the current state of the system, was a manual one. Trial and error over the years had failed to produce any more effective method, at a reasonable cost, than the one of using spread sheets described earlier in this chapter. The computer, up to that time, had not been of much help because the many data sources and inflexible format did not lend themselves to batch use that was effective in the problem context.

Variable Operations Required

The most appropriate information was not known until the problem-solving process was actually under way. Therefore instructions, specifying the desired subset of information to be used, could not be set up ahead of time. Similarly it was not feasible to have prespecified manipulation designed to produce a certain report, since the relevant information and report were not known ahead of time, or if they were, they did not remain relevant for more than a few months.

Different Criteria

The criteria for selecting possible problems were not known until the moment of selection. The pattern of results and behavior actually experienced during the previous month helped to determine the criteria to be used in selecting possible problems. In part, then, these criteria unfold during the actual decision-making process.

Time Requirements

The size of the data-base imposed real limitations on the amount of time available for selection. All data were laid out on spread sheets and the process of comparing columns of numbers looking for significant differences required considerable time. The implications of a decision could not be traced through in under 20 minutes and it frequently took several hours. Even 20 minutes served as a very effective block to rational decision making!

Cognitive Limitations

Given the human brain's limited memory capacity for detail, the conceptualizing of the present state of affairs from long columns of numbers is an unsatisfactory process. The decision makers exhibited inconsistent behavior when they tried to do this, and any attempt to record partial results was so time-consuming it only aggravated the problem.

Implementation

The ability to implement a solution once it had been thought of was such a pedestrian and time-consuming process that the decision maker ceased to innovate with solutions and used the same standard approach every time. Thus, design became routine and was limited to one or two strategies only. There was no exploration or iteration of possible solutions.

Conceptualization

The manager was often lost in tables of figures and could not get himself far enough removed to gain perspective. Large quantities of numbers and limited human memory capacity are not conducive to good planning activity. There was no mechanism to encourage or enforce rigorous consistent decision making.

Large Quantity of Computation

Similar to the data problems in 2, Exhibit 4–7, the large quantity of data was further aggravated by the greater complexity of the manipulation. In this design phase of the decision-making process, the manipulation had to be able to portray the impact of an alternative on the variables involved and do this into the future. This meant more computation and a greater complexity of computation than that experienced in 2, Exhibit 4–7.

Variable Operations Required

As in 2, Exhibit 4–7, it was not possible to prespecify the relevant data involved. This meant that the managers had to do this as the problem-solving process progressed. To look at several alternative design solutions for a problem involved several different sets of computations. These computations became known only as the implications of the previous alternative became clear.

Implications

With the problems identified in "Implementation" and "Large Quantity of Computation" above, it is clear that there was no reasonable way for the decision maker to see the implications of his decision on the other related variables. In short, he could not readily determine the impact of a proposed solution.

Solution Space

With the time and capacity problems under "Design" the decision maker did not have the capacity to explore the theoretical solution space. In fact, he was "satisficing" by taking the first acceptable solution—the only one he generated. His choice was thus a simple "go," "no go" situation.

Multiple Criteria

If he had had more than one solution, which in practice was usually *not* the case, there would be a further problem of determining the ranking of each solution with respect to a variety of criteria. This would impose considerable manipulative requirements.

Comparison of Alternatives

Due to the multidimensionality of the problem, comparison among solutions was complex. Hence, the conceptualization issue again became important. With the old process there was typically only one solution, so the comparison issue was effectively not a problem.

CONCLUSIONS

From the extensive observational period of the "old process" it became obvious that the above list contains most of the principal bottlenecks in that process. These were not caused by inability on the part of the managers involved, but rather were an inevitable result of the problem and the process needed for its solution with the technology then available. The next chapter provides some specific detail on this framework and the former decision process.

Chapter 5

FORMER PROCESS IN THE CONTEXT
OF THE FRAMEWORK

CHAPTERS 3 AND 4 HAVE DISCUSSED A FRAMEWORK within which to look at management decision making and have examined the process used by the managers before the introduction of the Management Decision Systems (MDS).

	Intelligence	Design	Choice
Generation	1	4	7
Manipulation	2	5	8
Selection	3	6	9

As was discussed in Chapter 3, it has been suggested that the process of decision making involves three major steps and within each of these there are three substeps. This chapter is concerned with exploring the nature of each of these nine cells in the framework and with the likely impact of the MDS on them. The "potential impact" section in the discussion of each cell provides some speculation as to the kind of impact one might expect from use of the MDS. This is provided in the context of the problem to make the uses of the MDS as specific as possible.

The project is, after all, concerned with the impact of interactive display systems on management, particularly decisions made by line managers. In order to see what this impact actually is, it is necessary to have a clear, sharp, model of the process as it was. Only then can one be sure of the impact the new system has made. The discussion that follows is designed to provide an understanding of the problem as it was characterized for analysis.

Cell 1. Intelligence/Generation

This cell, or portion of the process, is concerned with gaining access to all the raw data the managers need when they search the environment for potential problems. In a typical business situation these data are normally generated in the course of some natural function of the business and are held somewhere in the organization. For example, dollar figures on total sales can be obtained as a by-product of the invoicing function. The data-base for this intelligence/generation subphase should include all data necessary to identify and solve the problem. This would include the internal (to the organization) formal data, as well as the external (generated outside the organization) data that are relevant and economical to collect. It is useful to have these data sets in some form of computer compatible medium so they can be searched and dealt with without manual intervention.[1]

Former Process

In the old system the decision maker received computer-based data and transcribed these data into a form (Exhibit 4–5) he had found useful in the past. His data were manually transcribed from a series of computer-based runs which arrived within the first five working days of every month (see Appendix D). Other information was received from other manual reports and put on the form. In summary the information available to the managers was as follows:

---

[1] This problem is discussed in considerable detail by Jim Emery (28) in his work on data-bases.

Data	*Source*
Actual Sales—Current Year	Computer Print-Out (CPO)
Actual Sales—Last Year	Manual Report (MR)
Previous Forecast (Last Month)	MR
Current Forecast	Working Form
Sales Objectives	MR
Sales Forecast (Exponential Forecast)	CPO
Production, Actual	CPO
Production, Planned	MR
Inventory, Factory	CPO
Inventory, Total	CPO
Inventory, Objective	MR

All of this was fixed information which the managers used regularly in making their decisions. The managers also had, but did not write down, an entire month of activity in their own minds relating to unusual events or conditions in the past month. All this latter informal, and partially external, information was left unrecorded.

As described in the previous chapter, most of the formal information necessary for this particular problem was in the central computer center's data-base. This information was present and much of it updated on a real-time basis, although the data necessary in this case were month-end summaries and hence *not* dependent on the real-time aspects.

Potential Impact

It was expected that the principal impact of the MDS in this area would be one of time. In this specific case the time taken to bring the raw data to the decision makers could be speeded up by making extra computer runs unnecessary and by removing the necessity of physically moving the data (on printed forms) from the various geographical locations to the central headquarters.

Other than time, the MDS would not be expected to affect this process of generating information for the manipulation subphase. In the old and the new process, the managers' data-base was fairly complete. Therefore, the new system was deliberately designed to provide exactly the same quantity of raw data. The size of the data-base was unchanged during the experiment in the two systems.

The availability of informal, random type of information that was received by the managers would, almost by definition, not be affected by the MDS.

Cell 2. Intelligence/Manipulation

This cell is concerned with the processing of raw data through some appropriate framework to provide information for the selection subphase. This phase is one of generating clues from the raw data, clues that suggest possible problem areas. This is normally necessary, since raw data do not provide much information to the user. In general, manipulation to find clues can take any one of at least three forms:

(1) Deviations
(2) Trends
(3) Experimentation

Processing the raw data through one of these three general frameworks produces output which can be helpful to managers in identifying problem areas.

(1) Deviations: By comparing the raw data, suitably aggregated, to a budget or some other predetermined model it is possible to detect deviations from normal, or expected, performance. This can be done with financial or nonfinancial data, with any aggregation or comparison appropriate to the problem.

(2) Trends: By processing data through one of several possible analytical models, such as linear regression, it is possible to identify trends, or long-term patterns, in the data.

(3) Experimentation: In working closely with the data one can become sufficiently familiar with them to notice interesting peculiarities—these can then be examined in some organized fashion to determine if they are of importance. The significant feature with this type of manipulation is that there is no predetermined set of calculations or comparisons—the possible paths of analysis are only discerned as the data or problem are closely examined in the process of solving this problem.

All three of these methods of generating clues are time-consuming if the data-base is large. They become ineffective if the data-base is large and has to be dealt with manually. With computer-based data, however, "programmed" decisions are amenable to solution with batch-processing computers in the first and second methods above. This is assuming that it is possible to establish decent criteria as to what constitutes a significant deviation, and so forth. Similarly with programmed decisions in which trends are a relevant factor it will often be possible to analyze the data and determine the trend on a programmed, or predetermined, basis.

In the "nonprogrammed" situation, however, it is possible to use these methods only to the extent that *elements* of the problem are "programmed." A computer operated in the batch mode is not likely to have the flexibility necessary to do an adequate job with these three types of manipulation in a nonprogrammed decision. The reasons for this are straightforward—being a nonprogrammed decision it is not possible to establish criteria, or indeed the specific data, in advance. Hence, these criteria have to be specified at the time the user is actually involved with the decision-making process. To generate useful clues requires some form of interactive communication with the machine; this tends to exclude batch-processing modes of operation. The interaction can be fairly formal and rigid in the first and second types (deviations and trends) but should be very flexible for the third, experimentation.

It is this experimentation and "discovery" activity that has the potential of providing considerable augmentation for the "intelligence" phase of problem solving. The innovative, creative decision maker is the one who is able to recognize hitherto unrealized patterns of causation and capitalize on them; an interactive terminal system should have considerable impact on this activity.

Former Process

The old process required the MPM (or his staff) to transcribe data by hand to a form (Exhibit 4–5), that he had designed and found useful. This form made it easier for him to see points of significance in the data. The form required some manipulation since the monthly data on the form were cumulative and there were also some percentages taken. The cumulative figures provided performance to date and expected year-end data, all of which were compared to budgeted data and last year's performance as described in Chapter 4. The time taken to transcribe and cumulate was large, about five to seven days of work, or some 30% of the total time. The final figures were not in a flexible format; when changes were made the number was erased and the relevant impact recalculated by adding machine. For example, if the current forecast was changed for July (see Exhibit 4–5), then the remainder of the months had to be erased and the new cumulative figures calculated and inserted for each month. This was a rather time-consuming process and not one that was conducive to experimentation with different values. If it had been computerized on a batch basis, the process would have been no better as the time saved from manual manipulation would be spent preparing the input and waiting for the results. All this manipulation (i.e., aggregate, reorganize, add in machine forecast) was designed to indicate the presence of any clues.

The manipulation subphase, then, should generate information that will be amenable to interpretation for clues to problems.

Potential Impact

The impact of the MDS on this subphase was expected to be considerable. The interaction, convenience, and flexibility of a remote terminal seemed to be necessary to overcome the bottlenecks in the former process and provide access to the necessary power. The ability to employ relevant models to filter the raw data and generate clues to potential problems is an important attribute of the system. Interaction between the manager and system allows him to specify what he feels are the appropriate data, time period, models, and so forth. He can then organize these components so that they provide him with information. The visual aspects were not expected to be of great significance beyond the features of convenience and speed. With a nonprogrammed problem, the use and combination of different analytical frameworks are functions of the state-of-the-search-process, the nature of the data, and the problem at hand. Each framework requires its own manipulation. None of these is predetermined; in fact, they are only known as the process proceeds. Hence the user should have the ability to specify manipulative procedures at the moment of analysis. This is possible with an interactive device. To be useful, such a device has to be flexible, simple to operate, and exhibit the other characteristics discussed in Chapter 2. It is access to the data-base and computational power of the machine that is likely to be important, so that any terminal that can handle the interaction involved in the input and output, would be adequate for this purpose.

The MDS, as a terminal, is of central importance to this subphase and it was expected to change the process considerably. It was felt that it would have the following effects:

(1) Cut the time for manipulation to such an extent that other interested managers would take part in the search process.
(2) Increase the number and types of manipulations used.
(3) Allow greater flexibility in the values used for the parameters in any one manipulation.
(4) Increase the investigation of patterns of performance identified by any manager involved as being atypical.
(5) Result in change in the problem "search" process, a change toward greater depth of search.

Cell 3. Intelligence/Selection

The selection cell in the framework is where the output of the manipulation process is examined for clues that may identify problems. In the programmable case, as was mentioned, this is a trivial problem as long as the criteria for "what is the problem?" are known and specified—then any variations from this can be identified by the machine, in batch mode if necessary. In the nonprogrammable case this is more difficult since almost by definition there is unlikely to be a clear set of criteria. For this reason the selection and manipulation are iterated several times. The first pass through the manipulation process may result in the identification of an almost normal set of data. This might then be examined from another standpoint (i.e., some different manipulation designed to bring out some other characteristic of the data). Depending on the results of this second examination some further manipulation could be done, or this area could be considered a problem and left for the second major phase of the decision-making process. Thus by "adding" together all clues, and searching around for new clues, one gets an aggregate picture of the different areas. Then the decision has to be made as to whether there are enough indications to classify the area as a problem. This latter is an intuitive, subjective process in which various heuristics are used to perform the selection procedures. The decision maker has a set of rules of thumb (largely undefined) as to what constitutes acceptable performance. The decision to classify the area as a problem sets it aside for further investigation. If he is satisfied the area is normal, he can pass on to the next area; if he is uncertain, he can return to the manipulation subphase and process the data through a different framework.

Former Process

Under the old system the managers looked at the tables that had been generated and by comparing numbers within columns and end-of-year cumulative totals they decided whether or not they felt there was a problem. Depending on how the numbers "looked," the managers had to decide what to compare and what they regarded as a problem. This was an intuitive process and they were unable initially to verbalize the criteria they used. For example, on one item they might have regarded performance at 10% below objective with three months' supply of inventory to be a problem, and on another item this might have been completely acceptable.

Thus all three groups, marketing, manufacturing and staff, looked at performance data (as described earlier) that had been processed in a manner which they had found in the past to be convenient. In addition, all three groups knew of other conditions, either specifically because they were intracompany problems that they had been forced to deal with, or else the "fringe of consciousness"[2] type of problem that was triggered by looking at the data. "Fringe of consciousness" describes the situation where a specific element of data triggers the recollection of some specific event

---

[2] See Dreyfus (25).

which either was, or will become, a problem. In the old process this selection of possible problems was done initially (see description in Chapter 4) by the MPM alone, who then proceeded to devise a solution. At a later point the others involved examined his solutions and suggested further modifications, as well as identifying other items they regarded as problems. The MPM then adjourned the meeting in order to take the time to do the manipulation and see if the suggested problems were in fact legitimate.

Potential Impact

The MDS was expected to have a considerable impact on this subphase. A typewriter terminal would have provided the necessary interaction but would have been intolerably slow in producing the output in a form useful for the selection process. With a visual device providing very fast graphical representation it becomes possible to display large quantities of information in a compact, meaningful, and easily understood form. This graphical representation could be central to the intelligence/selection process which involves a form of pattern-recognition, in essence visualizing relationships among the data. Displaying the information in the readily understood form of graphs could permit fast assimilation of the variables and their interrelationships.

This characteristic of graphs is not, of course, unique to computer-driven displays, but with the other terminal characteristics of interaction with the tube-face and the rapid displaying of new graphs, one could end up with a very powerful device for this subphase. The heuristic process of selection would probably not be affected—that would still remain largely undefined but the MDS would allow those involved to "see" the possible problem area from several standpoints. Hence, the MDS might be expected to:

(1) Reduce the time spent in meetings concerned with the "Intelligence" phase.
(2) Permit examination of those items selected for investigation more thoroughly than before. This would involve more displays of several combinations of variables; essentially, iteration through Phases 2 and 3.

(3) Make it possible for the MM, who knows the marketplace best, to take part in the problem search process. (His interest would be maintained and the time involved would be short.)

(4) Provide "information" from the display more readily than from the previous process.

CELL 4. DESIGN/GENERATION

	Intelligence	Design	Choice
Generation	1	4	7
Manipulation	2	5	8
Selection	3	6	9

The fourth cell in the framework deals with the initial aspects of the solution design process. Generation, invention, or design of possible solutions require as bases a clear understanding of the problem. Hence, the first step is to follow through on Phase 3 (Intelligence/Selection) and ascertain that the problem is understood. Examination of the problem area may be required again from several different standpoints. This invention, or generation, of design possibilities is the creative part of the decision-making process. Creativity, to be useful, must be channeled in the right direction and exploited in a consistent fashion. The process of forcing some rigor and consistency into the decision-making process is the subject of a book by Tregoe and Kepner.[3] One of the points they stress[4] is that it is essential to have a clear understanding of the precise nature of the problem before trying to find a solution. The creation of a solution is a function of human ingenuity and, in the case of a nonprogrammable type of problem, it is unlikely that any other single source will yield the final solution in the immediate future. Thus, in a programmable problem, it may be possible to solve the problem and derive a satisfactory answer with some form of algorithm. In the nonprogrammable case, although algorithms may be involved, the solution is created by some original combination of algorithm and "insight." The

[3] See Tregoe and Kepner (80).
[4] *Ibid.*, p. 44.

Design/Generation cell, then, is concerned with clarifying the problem and inventing possible solutions.

Former Process

In the old process the MPM developed his understanding of the problem areas by complete immersion in the details. Transcription of data, aggregation and comparisons left him with a well-developed feel for the problem. The other managers involved did not have this same understanding. In fact, their understanding was generally limited to specific situations in which they had been involved and extreme conditions in the short run. The MPM did very little in the way of testing to see if his understanding of the problem was correct; he moved straight into the manipulation subphase by inserting a value to see if it would alleviate the problem. The MPM by-passed this searching, or invention, of design possibilities because his complete immersion in the detail during Phase 1 left him with what he felt was enough of a grasp to select a method of solution and a specific value.

Potential Impact

The MDS might be expected to have little or no impact on the creation of solutions but could have a considerable impact on the presentation and clarification of the problem area. The system could enable those involved to visualize the relationships between variables, in effect to see a representation of the information that could be quickly and easily grasped.

Examining the data from several standpoints with the MDS could provide all those involved with a good understanding of the problem in a short space of time. With a commonly understood problem the creation of a solution should be a less difficult task. Thus the decision makers would be more likely to select useful solutions at an earlier stage in the process. The ease of comprehension should allow other people to be involved and thus provide additional sources of informal information. In general, inventing possible solutions in the nonprogrammable case will tend to be a human function although the machine could well serve as a more effective and retentive memory for the results of previous implementation of certain solutions.

The creative thought, then, will be human. The MDS has the potential of an accurate memory device, so, to the extent that outcomes can be decently classified, it should be possible to check the "creative thought" to see if such an avenue had been successful in the past. Beyond this possible role, however, the system's only present function, albeit a significant one, would be to clarify the problem. Thus it could be expected that:

(1) Subphases 2 and 3 would involve a great many more manipulations and comparisons than the old process.
(2) Subphases 4, 5, and 6 would be cycled through several times for each identified problem in an attempt to design a more adequate solution.
(3) The managers involved would participate in the design process together.

Cell 5. Design/Manipulation

The design/manipulation phase is where specific values are processed through the appropriate framework. The results of this are then used in the design/selection subphase to see if they are an improvement on the previous solution. If there is no improvement, another set is tried. If certain elements are found to be less clear than before when examining the results of a manipulation, then the framework is changed and either the same, or another, set of values is processed. Having generated a possible solution, the values involved are tested out to see what impact the solution does have on the variables involved. The manipulation is carried out far enough so that information is generated for the selection subphase in which it is decided if the solution is acceptable. If it is not acceptable, then at least some information has been generated that may be of assistance in selecting the next inputs with which to enter the design/generation subphase. The cycle of design/generation/manipulation/selection ends with an apparently acceptable solution and the choice phase is entered. If the manipulation/selection subphases do not produce an acceptable solution, then the "generation" subphase is re-entered and a different value or framework is used to try to find an acceptable solution.

Former Process

The development of the design/manipulation occurred in the old process when the managers looked at the impact of a suggestion on the other items. If the impact was not satisfactory, they might make a gross order change (sufficiently conservative to be safe) and then rework the data to arrive at the new cumulative figures. This was a change based on their intuition alone and was not the result of experimentation. Thus, for example, if performance was very good in one model and as expected in the balance of the models, and the managers knew that an advertising promotion was coming up, then they would make an adjustment in forecasted sales for the period in question. As soon as this adjustment was implemented, they might find that the production facilities for the model and for the inventory levels in some warehouse had been violated. Hence, the solution would not be satisfactory, and they would have to go back and readjust it to reflect these violations.

In the old system the manipulation was a laborious process of recalculating cumulative totals or reallocating a change in the aggregate among a variety of models. As discussed below (see Cell 6), this was not a process that was repeated if it was at all possible to avoid it. It was a time-consuming and tedious task.

Potential Impact

The impact of the MDS on this subphase could be significant. Access to manipulative power at this point in the decision-making process should be of considerable assistance. It would become possible to test different solutions, seeing the impact of a suggested solution on the other variables involved. This ability to perceive the expected impact of a possible decision on a range of variables more or less immediately and then have the option of testing another solution, is a significant feature of an interactive system. This speed and convenience could have several advantages in the process. As in the intelligence phase the reduction in time should be sufficiently great that there would be a willingness to try more values for any given framework. In addition, the MPM can be joined through the whole process by the others involved, thus making it more of a group process of all those with information to contribute.

The MDS with its flexible access to manipulative power should:

(1) Allow a greater number of "solutions" to be tested out, that is, solutions involving different variables.
(2) Allow several different values for the same variable to be tested.

Cell 6. Design/Selection

This selection phase is only concerned with screening the results of the design/manipulation subphase to determine if the output is acceptable. If the results are not acceptable the reasons are analyzed and the "generation" subphase re-entered. "Acceptable" is not a term with any very precise meaning and is therefore appropriate for a nonprogrammable problem. There is no one set of criteria that can always be used, and hence no good way of deciding whether a set of values constitutes an "acceptable" solution. In the long run, the terminal system may be of help in trying to develop complex criteria for such multivalued problems. With the storage and display capabilities presently available, it may be possible to display solutions along several dimensions and thus do a more thorough job of evaluation. It is not suggested that this evaluation will become automated, but with the manipulative and display capabilities of the system the decision maker has the option of easily looking at a great many more variables than before.

Former Process

In the old system this selection process was largely intuitive. The managers checked to make sure that they had not violated any of the constraints of which they were aware, but beyond that their "sense" of the adequacy of a solution was all that they employed to decide if it was satisfactory. The first satisfactory solution under the old process was taken as *the* answer, normally to both the Design and Choice phases.

Potential Impact

The impact of the MDS of this subphase could be high, since the decision makers have the option of looking at their solution along several different dimensions. Without the display device, it would not be practical to display the impact of a solution on a variety of variables. The time involved would be long and the number of solutions too high. An additional benefit in displaying several dimensions of the problem might be that this could ultimately result in the development of multidimensional criteria. Such understanding could then lead to a rationalization of the presently unidentified criteria used by the manager, essentially moving the problem back toward the programmed sphere.

The display characteristics could be of importance here; it is possible, with the MDS, to display the impact of various solutions on the screen. Looking at the pattern of results in rapid sequence allows one to compare along any dimension that seems important. Thus, the impact of the MDS could be that:

(1) Several modifications would be tried with each initial "solution."
(2) More than one satisfactory solution would be generated and held over for the next phase.
(3) The managers would develop a more explicit set of criteria as to what constitutes an acceptable solution.

Cell 7. Choice/Generation

	Intelligence	Design	Choice
Generation	1	4	7
Manipulation	2	5	8
Selection	3	6	9

The seventh cell in the framework is the choice/generation subphase. This is concerned with the provision of potential solutions from which to select a course of action. As was suggested in subphases 4, 5, and 6, these solutions are generated in the design phase by iteration through the three subphases until a reasonable number of acceptable solutions are generated. This cell then is concerned with the control of steps 4, 5, and 6. This problem of determining whether enough reasonable alternatives have been generated from the previous three steps is a complex one. It is the problem of strategy for problem solution and determining whether enough information has been generated from previous alternatives or whether further trials will yield greater insight.

Former Process

With nonprogrammed decisions that are complex or involve large amounts of time, there is a tendency for decision makers to behave in a "satisficing" fashion[5]—that is, they accept the first satisfactory solution that they happen upon. This well-documented phenomenon is quite apparent in the old process where the managers stopped their search promptly at the first reasonably satisfactory answer, satisfactory in this case being a situation where no constraints were violated and the managers felt "happy" with the solution. There was little evidence of any consideration being given to the possibility of testing another solution. The clerical and managerial time involved in choosing and executing another generation of a "Design" cycle was too great to encourage innovation.

Potential Impact

With the new process there would be little or no penalty in time or effort attached to trying out different values in the same framework. Such behavior is in no way optimizing behavior but it would be a step in the right direction and it could improve the quality of the decision.

The impact here could be high, as the option of generating several solutions was simply not open in any practical way under the former system. This is a significant option because it provides the manager with a range of solutions; this means that he could

---

[5] See Simon (42).

have the opportunity of selecting the best of those offered. In general, it seems fairly clear that this would in turn mean the possibility of an improvement of performance. Another significant impact here, however, could be that with this capability of generating more solutions, the managers would be tempted to try new and different combinations and examine their impacts. They might also, perhaps, develop other rules of thumb as they see the effects of changes in certain variables. All of this activity could lead to a heightened understanding and a greater realization of the nature of the variables involved and some of the cause and effect relationships. This understanding might come sufficiently rapidly and easily so that others than just the MPM could benefit from this and play a more significant part in the whole process. Thus, it might be expected that:

(1) The managers would repeat the design phase more than once.
(2) The managers would generate several alternative solutions.

CELL 8. CHOICE/MANIPULATION

This cell is where the various alternatives that have been generated are put into some kind of a framework, or otherwise manipulated, so that they are in a form that is appropriate for the selection phase.

In nonprogrammable problems this is difficult as there is no simple criterion for choice and it is hard to make up a set that will always be applicable. What is required is a flexible manipulation system that permits easy selection of framework, time periods, or variables so that the multidimensional comparison can take place.

Former Process

The old system had very little flexibility; when there was a choice of more than one alternative, the solution was made by the managers on the basis of their intuition, although there was some comparative reference made between *a* new solution and the previous (original) solution. There was no comparison between alternative courses of action since they were normally not available. Hence the only form of manipulation used in the old system was the juxtaposition of two numbers and a mental comparison.

Potential Impact

The impact here could be significant if the decision makers have frameworks which require manipulation before selection. Under these conditions it would be helpful to have the system do the processing. The manipulation could consist of recall and display—nontrivial if there is a large volume of data, but nevertheless not highly dependent on an MDS. Or it could consist of executing complex decision models that have been built up from relevant algorithms that reflect those criteria the managers are able to make explicit. This latter form of manipulation makes greater use of the MDS capabilities.

Thus this phase has potential for high impact if the problem should be such that manipulation at this stage generates additional information of a comparative nature between solutions. In many nonprogrammable problems it would not seem as if further manipulation would help since the criteria are largely undefined. The MDS, however, would always be helpful in dealing with high volumes of data, reducing them to understandable form, thus allowing a clear understanding of the alternatives in the choice/selection process.

CELL 9. CHOICE/SELECTION

This cell is concerned with final selection of one course of action. The various alternatives are manipulated to allow the best possible comparison. The comparison having been made, a particular course of action is chosen.

The managers did not do this under the old system since they had only one alternative. In the new system several alternatives can be displayed; this allows some comparison before selection. It was not expected that there would be much impact here, however, since there were no formal criteria established against which the managers could select a solution. Computer selection would be adequate in principle if one could get a list of criteria and show the alternatives in terms of these.

However, computer selection would be clearly impossible unless enough criteria could be identified, measured, and weighed. The manager, then, could be expected to continue his present heuristic type of selection procedures. The impact, therefore, of the MDS on this subphase would be slight.

CONCLUSIONS

The discussion of the former process, in the context of the nine-celled framework was designed to provide some understanding of the framework and of the decision process involved in the experimental setting. Although very simple, the framework does provide some structure for what would otherwise be a rather amorphous process. Given the decision situation, the bottlenecks currently involved and the characteristics of the terminal system, it was possible to make some suggestions as to the likely impact of the system. These have been raised in the context of the framework to make the possible impact as clear as possible. Evidence on the actual impact is given in Appendix D and discussed in Chapters 7 and 8.

Chapter 6

IMPLEMENTATION

TWO ASPECTS OF THE IMPLEMENTATION of the Management Decision System are considered in the material that follows. The first section describes the system in operation. A series of diagrams, each with a brief description, is used to provide the reader with a sense of the way in which the system operates in this problem environment.

The second section of the chapter discusses the strategy used for the design and implementation of the system as well as the various phases of the experimentation process. Included in this section are some observations on particular implementation problems and a reference to the costs involved.

SYSTEM DESCRIPTION

Introduction

There are some general points to be made concerning the displays involved before discussing the diagrams themselves. The first of these is the role of graphical information and the second the macro structure of the displays involved.

In Chapter 2 it was pointed out that display terminals with graphical capability were thought to have potential for managerial use and it is this graphical, or vector, capability that is one of the important features. This graphical feature may affect the *information* content of the raw data but it does not in this case affect the quantity or quality of the data available. Care was taken to ensure that the data input to this decision remained constant. Data in this instance are to be carefully differentiated from information. In order to examine the impact of the MDS in as stable an environment as possible, it seemed reasonable to allow the user access to only that data he had before the change. Thus the type of data remains constant; however, the way in which the data are represented and the way in which they are handled change considerably. In short, the managers have access to the same numbers that they had before. These data become information when they are relevant to a particular part of the decision process; thus the data are the same, but the information content of the data is considerably changed by this system.

In this instance the change to graphical form is only possible through the use of computer-driven displays since there is no other economical way of drawing graphs except by manual or "Calcomp plotter" methods. A mechanical paper and pen-plotting device (such as Calcomp), while admirably suited for its original purpose, cannot be said to be interactive. The interactive capability requires speed of response (the Calcomp is slow), and the ability to provide a meaningful stimulus to the system from the display itself, that is, the cathode-ray tube and light-pen provide an understandable message to the computer without further specification by the user. Thus the change to interactive graphical representation is only feasible with a computer-driven display and this is the only change that was provided to the user. That is, he was provided with a display system capable of performing the above functions and asked to go ahead and solve his problems.

The Management Decision System at the time of this experiment had three principal displays: the Specifications, Graphical, and Reconcile displays. Each of these was appropriate for a particular part of the decision process and each has a control point which can be hit with the light-pen to allow the user to move from one to the other. Within each display there are three categories of control point:

(1) Data Control: a series of light-buttons which permit the user to request any further data to be displayed.

(2) Manipulative Control: a series of light-buttons which allow the user to request computational power to recalculate the impact of a change on the related variables.

(3) Movement Control: these enable the user to look at another graph, a different time span or similar movement through the data.

These options, under light-pen control, provide the user with a simple, flexible and powerful means of support in this decision-making process. The control points are in the user's terminology and are designed to provide support for him and his particular style of decision making. The system is flexible because the user can jump to any part of the system and have access to any data that he feels are relevant at the particular moment of decision. It is powerful because the user has access to the full capability of the computer and data-base and any formal models that he wishes to use.

The significant change in data representation, then, is the use of graphs. In this type of environment it was felt that cumulative graphs conveyed more meaningful information than noncumulative graphs, largely because the users were always concerned with performance over time. However, both forms of graph are available to the user; the noncumulative graph has the traditional structure. The cumulative graph (see Exhibit 6–1) has a number of modifications which turned out to be useful. These are mentioned below.

In the past, this graphical form shown in Exhibit 6–1 had been found highly effective in conveying information. However, it was not a feasible operating tool for anything other than occasional presentations, since there was so much effort involved in drawing the graph manually.

The information content conveyed by this form of display is quite high. For example, if one examines Exhibit 6–2 and tries to determine the status of performance this year, one can ask the question,

EXHIBIT 6–1

CARR CHART—EXAMPLE *

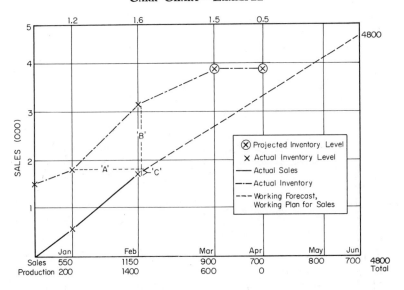

* See Notes for explanation.

NOTES: The following points can be made with respect to the Carr Chart implemented on the system:

1. The x axis is nonlinear, the distances between months being proportional to the seasonal factor for the item being graphed. An item selling in accordance with its seasonal pattern will, therefore, be a straight line.

2. The distance "B" represents production in February, the distance "B + C" represents inventory position as of February 28. The distance "A" represents the months of supply of inventory on hand given the projected sales. In this example 1.6 months' supply at the end of February.

3. The symbols ⊗ mark expected inventory status given the present production plans. For example, there is no production planned for this item in April.

4. The intercept with the right-hand axis, or any other month gives the period-to-date cumulative total. In this example the six-month cumulative is 4,800. Below each month appear the actual monthly (noncumulative) data used.

5. Changes in the slope of the line indicate changes in the rate of sales, or whatever the line represents.

6. Obviously one can plot as many lines as are useful on the same graph. For example, Sales Objective, Last Year's Sales, and so forth.

EXHIBIT 6–2
SAMPLE PERFORMANCE DATA—TABULAR*

A (Noncumulative)

	J	F	M	A	M	J	J	A	S
Actual	3,400	2,600	2,400	1,800					
Forecast					1,700	2,000	2,100	1,700	1,500
Objective	2,900	2,500	2,200	1,800	2,000	3,800	3,400	2,800	2,200
Last Year	2,500	2,000	1,800	1,500	1,700	3,500	3,300	2,700	1,800
Inventory	4,600	4,000	4,800	5,200	5,500	6,800	—	—	—
Production	2,200	1,700	3,000	2,400	1,900	2,100	—	—	—

B (Cumulative)

	J	F	M	A	M	J	J	A	S
Actual	3,400	6,000	8,200	10,000					
Forecast					11,600	13,500	15,800	17,500	19,000
Objective	2,900	5,400	7,200	8,800	10,800	13,800	17,200	20,000	22,200
Last Year	2,500	4,500	6,300	7,800	9,500	12,000	15,300	18,000	19,800
Inventory	4,600	4,000	4,800	5,200	5,500	6,800	—	—	—
Production	2,200	1,700	3,000	2,400	1,900	2,100	—	—	—

* See text for explanation.

is everything proceeding according to plan? This would include such things as performance relative to last year and the objective, control of inventory, and control of similar problems in production. After trying to determine this with Exhibit 6–2, if one does the same thing with Exhibit 6–3, then it becomes readily apparent that the graph (be it cumulative or otherwise) is very much more comprehensible, both in terms of time taken and the ability to detect trends and patterns. This point is discussed at a more general level elsewhere but it is mentioned again here in the context of a specific example to demonstrate the nature of the phenomena being discussed.

System Operation

The user can operate the system from any location convenient to him. The telephone lines are all that are required to connect the terminal with the central computer. The system is activated by typing in a five-letter code which brings a Specifications display onto the screen. The user then specifies with the light-pen what he wishes to see. From this point on, the light-pen is used for all inputs except new values of the variables; these inputs are made on the keyboard.

The twenty-two inch screen can be easily viewed by three or four people in normal room lighting, and response time to a request varies between one and ten seconds depending on the nature of the request. The user typically hits two or three control points and then spends several minutes analyzing the graph the system responds with. He then tries one or two more changes and when satisfied enters the data onto the permanent files.

Hard-copy print-out is obtained by requesting from the terminal a printed version of the data-base. This is printed at the main computer center and sent by mail. There is no technical reason why this could not come off a teletype at the users' location. However, these particular users, when finished with their process, have no urgent need of a permanent record. A Polaroid camera is also available and used occasionally as an inexpensive and rapid form of hard-copy.

To provide some specific detail on the way the first experimental system operated, there follows a series of diagrams each with a brief verbal description of the action taken by the user and an explanation of the resulting display. These diagrams use disguised data which are consistent with the actual experimental data.

Sample Performance Data—Graphical

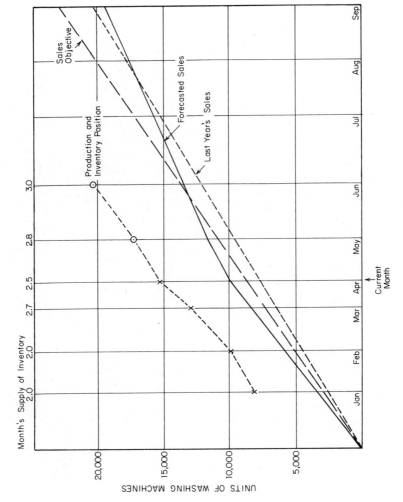

Figure 6.1: Display System for the MDS

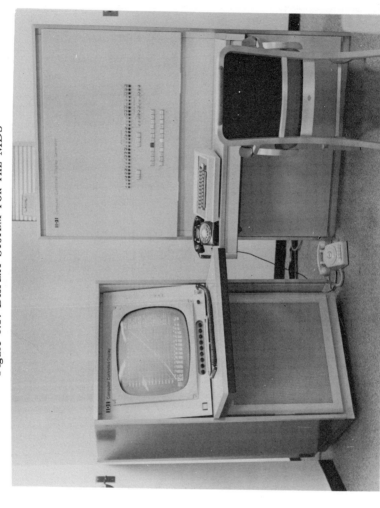

NOTE: Figure 6.1 is a photograph of the display system that was used in the experiment. It was built by Information Display, Inc.

Figure 6.2: Sample Output from the MDS

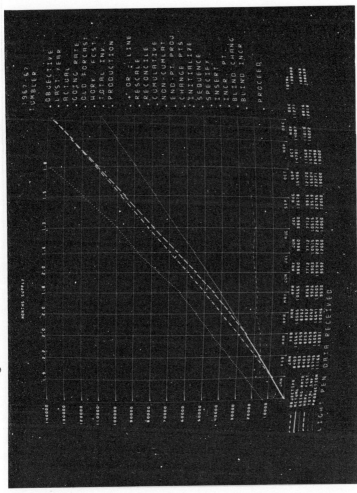

NOTE: This actual photograph of the screen provides a view of the system. For reasons of readability on this reduced scale, Figures 6.3–6.11 have been drawn in diagram form rather than photographed. These diagrams reproduce exactly the image on the screen as in this photograph.

Figure 6.3: Graph Specifications

DISPLAY FORMAT	DATA	AXIS	TIME			
GRAPH- CUMULATIVE	WASHERS	SEASONAL	JAN	1965	JAN	1965
	TUMBLERS	NORMAL	FEB	1966	FEB	1966
GRAPH- NON CUMULATIVE	AGITATORS		MAR	1967	MAR	1967
			APR	1968	APR	1968
RECONCILE	T - 100		MAY	1969	MAY	1969
	T - 200		JUN		JUN	
	T - 300		JUL		JUL	
	T - 500		AUG		AUG	
	T - 550		SEP		SEP	
			OCT		OCT	
	A - 100		NOV		NOV	
	A - 200		DEC		DEC	
	A - 300					
	A - 400					
	A - 500					
	A - 600					
	A - 700					
	A - 800					
	A - 900					
PROCEED						

(See Notes on page 89.)

Figure 6.3: GRAPH SPECIFICATIONS

The display in Figure 6.3 is obtained by the user's typing in a call request on the keyboard. This is the Specifications display for graphical representation of data. One item from each column is "hit" with the light-pen to specify the type of graph the user wants.

For example, the following points would be "hit" to produce the next graph. The order is irrelevant, with the exception that "PROCEED" must be last: GRAPH-CUMULATIVE; TUMBLERS; SEASONAL; JAN; 1967; DEC; 1967; PROCEED. (All displays use sample data.)

Figure 6.4: END-POINT PROJECT

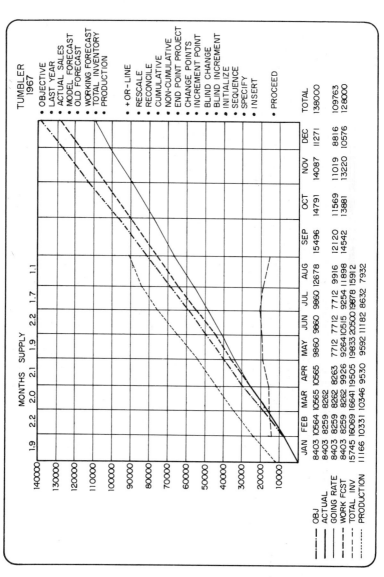

(See Notes on page 92.)

Figure 6.5: Change Points

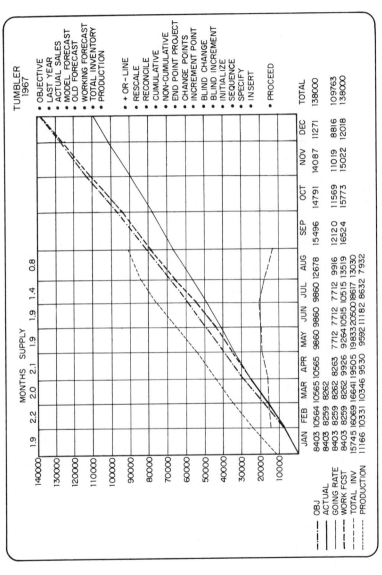

(See Notes on page 92.)

Figure 6.4: END-POINT PROJECT

Having looked at Figure 6.4 perhaps the user does not like the working forecast (present sales plan) for the tumblers, presently set for 128,000 units by December 31. Instead he decides to expand merchandising in the last half of the year and feels he can meet his objective of 138,000 by December 31. He wants to expand his sales rate, starting in JUL, in order to meet his objective by year end.

This is done by hitting the following control points in any sequence:

(a) WORKING FORECAST and END-POINT PROJECT (to indicate which manipulation is to be carried out on which variable).
(b) JUL (to indicate the starting month of the projection).
(c) An ending value to project to, in this case 138,000. This is typed on the keyboard.
(d) PROCEED (this results in the next picture).

Figure 6.5: CHANGE POINTS

The display in Figure 6.5 shows that there was only .8 month's supply of inventory on August 31 (small number at very top of graph). If the manager regarded this as unsatisfactory, he might change his production plan. In this example, the following control points were hit to generate the next picture:

(a) PRODUCTION; CHANGE POINTS (to identify the variable and the manipulation).
(b) AUG (to identify month).
(c) Type in new value (e.g., 18,000 for August).
(d) PROCEED.
(e) Repeat for September and October.

If INCR. PT. (add or substract an increment to a point) had been used, then the difference of 10,068 (18,000–7,932) would be typed.

Figure 6.6: RECONCILE

The new picture that is generated in Figure 6.6 has, obviously, a new production line. In addition, the month's supply has been recalculated and a new Total Inventory line plotted (bottom of screen).

If the manager now wanted to check this with last year's sales, he could bring those data on the screen by hitting the following control points:

(a) Data-control point LAST YEAR.
(b) Manipulation point + or − LINE.
(c) PROCEED.

Figure 6.6: RECONCILE

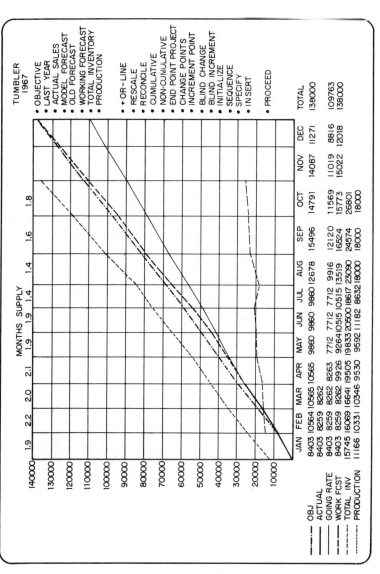

(See Notes on page 92.)

Figure 6.7: Last Year's Sales

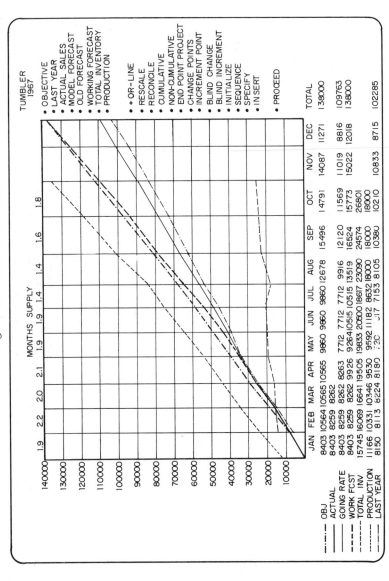

(See Notes on page 96.)

Figure 6.8: Reconcile Specifications

	FROM	TO
	JAN	JAN
	FEB	FEB
	MAR 1966	MAR 1966
	APR 1967	APR 1967
	MAY 1968	MAY 1968
	JUN 1969	JUN 1969
	JUL	JUL
	AUG	AUG
	SEP	SEP
	OCT	OCT
	NOV	NOV
	DEC	DEC

WASHER: TO: TUMBLER, AGITATOR

TUMBLER: TO: MODELS

AGITATOR: TO: MODELS

SALES   PRODUCTION

PROCEED

(See Notes on page 96.)

Figure 6.7: LAST YEAR'S SALES

Referring to Figure 6.7, if the Tumbler was now regarded as satisfactory, then the manager might want to see how he stood in relation to the Tumbler models. He then hits the RECONCILE and PROCEED control points. (See Figure 6.8 for the display results.)

Figure 6.8: RECONCILE SPECIFICATIONS

In Figure 6.8, one item from each column is selected with the light-pen. A choice is then made between sales and production. If the following were hit, the next picture would appear: TUMBLER: MODELS; JAN; 1967; DEC; 1967; SALES; PROCEED.

Figure 6.9: SALES RECONCILIATION

The user (see Figure 6.9) might wish to remove the discrepancies between the sales plan for the models and the sales plan for the aggregate, Tumblers, as follows:

(1) Take the difference in May of 709 units and spread it through all models in proportion to their present relationship. This is done by using the light-pen to select: MAY; RATIO; PROCEED.

The May column of the display would then look as in Figure 6.10.

(2) The user might then wish to change the difference in June by leaving the T-1 as is, and ratioing the difference into all the remaining models. This is done as follows:

With the light-pen, select

(a) The number, 3,643 (T-1 in June).
(b) FREEZE.
(c) RATIO.
(d) PROCEED.

The "June" column would then look as in Figure 6.10.

(3) He might then deal with July through December by deciding that the "Total" of the models was more reasonable than the Tumbler totals. This would simply involve changing the Tumbler number (10,515) to equal the Total (10,719).

The light-pen is used as follows:

(a) 10,515 (Select the number in Tumbler and July).
(b) CHANGE-PTS (enter 10,719).
(c) Repeat for each month.
(d) PROCEED.

The display would then look as in Figure 6.10.

Figure 6.9: SALES RECONCILIATION

1967   TUMBLER : MODELS

	JAN	FEB	MAR	APR	MAY	JUN	JUL	AUG	SEP	OCT	NOV	DEC	TOTAL
T-1	2764	3126	2896	3702	3084	3643	4279	5117	6032	7258	6973	5441	54315
T-2	2574	2664	2646	2686	2700	3140	2925	2064	1053	309	207	207	23175
T-3	2763	2323	2584	3116	2661	3352	2686	2049	1147	382	114	207	23384
T-4	0	0	0	0	0	0	328	2405	5131	5297	6032	4288	23481
T-5	0	0	0	0	0	0	0	0	0	0	0	0	0
T-6	0	0	0	0	0	0	437	1440	2601	2405	2265	2405	11553
T-7	302	146	136	422	110	154	64	30	85	54	33	12	1548
TOTAL	8403	8259	8262	9926	8555	10289	10719	13105	16049	15705	15624	12560	137456
TUMBLERS	8403	8259	8262	9926	9264	10515	10515	13519	16524	15773	15022	12018	138000
DIFFERENCE	0	0	0	0	709	226	204	414	475	68	602	542	544

- PROCEED
- INSERT
- CHANGE-PTS

- INITIALIZE
- RATIO

- SPECIFY
- RETURN

- FINISH
- FREEZE

- REFRESH
- GRAPH

(See Notes on page 96.)

Figure 6.10: RECONCILE

	JAN	FEB	MAR	APR	MAY	JUN	JUL	AUG	SEP	OCT	NOV	DEC	TOTAL
1967						TUMBLER : MODELS							
T-1	2764	3126	2896	3702	3343	3643	4279	5117	6032	7258	6973	5441	54574
T-2	2574	2664	2646	2686	2927	3249	2925	2064	1053	309	207	207	23511
T-3	2763	2323	2584	3116	2884	3466	2686	2049	1147	382	114	207	23721
T-4	0	0	0	0	0	0	328	2405	5131	5297	6032	4288	23481
T-5	0	0	0	0	0	0	0	0	0	0	0	0	0
T-6	0	0	0	0	0	0	437	1440	2601	2405	2265	2405	11553
T-7	302	146	136	422	110	157	64	30	85	54	33	12	1551
TOTAL	8403	8259	8262	9926	9264	10515	10719	13105	16049	15705	15624	12560	138391
TUMBLERS	8403	8259	8262	9926	9264	10515	10719	13105	16049	15705	15624	12560	138391
DIFFERENCE	0	0	0	0	0	0	0	0	0	0	0	0	0

- PROCEED
- INSERT
- CHANGE-PTS
- INITIALIZE
- RATIO
- SPECIFY
- RETURN
- FINISH
- FREEZE
- REFRESH
- GRAPH

(See Notes on page 100.)

Figure 6.11: NONCUMULATIVE GRAPH

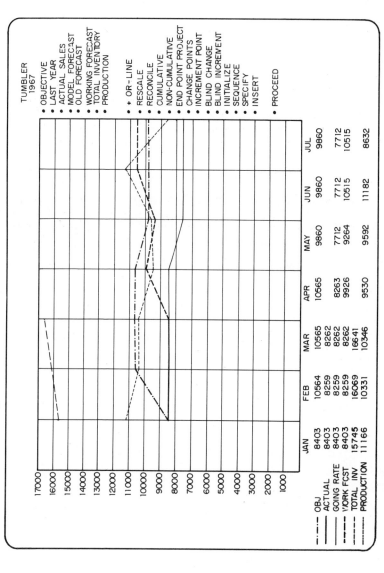

(See Notes on page 100.)

Figure 6.10: RECONCILE

The data (see Figure 6.10) are now entirely reconciled, the differences are all zero. If the user then wanted to look at a graph, he would select "Graph" on this display and he would then get a display as in "1" above.

If he selected the following points from the "SPECIFICATIONS" display in Figure 6.3, he would get the display in Figure 6.11: GRAPH-NON CUM; TUMBLER; NORMAL; JAN; 1967; JUL; 1967; PROCEED.

Figure 6.11: NONCUMULATIVE GRAPH

Figure 6.11 is simply an example of a noncumulative graph for a six-month time span. It is possible to display the cumulative version by selecting the "CUMULATIVE" control point and the "PROCEED." All control points listed in a display are legitimate options.

Design and Implementation

From the experience gained in implementing this system there are a few points in relation to the hardware, software and systems design that should be stressed. In general the experience of implementation seemed to be reminiscent of the early days (1955–58) of digital computers in the business field. All of the generalizations about the early experience with computers are perfectly applicable to the problems inherent in using visual terminals. Time estimates were too low, costs were higher than expected, and our biggest problems were with software. The hardware was less of a problem than the software and it has become clear that it is this latter region that will determine the speed with which visual display devices come into common use. We found the initial effort involved in putting the system on an operational footing was high and this was due almost entirely to the software development effort.

The hardware as well as the type of problem are new to the system's designers and managers involved. The type of application requires very heavy management involvement in the design phases as the system is being designed to support his particular decisions. This stress on the design of a management *decision* system as opposed to a traditional management *information* system is significant. It implies access to computational power, models, and the ability to readily organize data to support the decision-making process. The manager, as the user, has to be actively involved in the process.

Hardware

The implementation process clarified our ideas on the hardware characteristics, and these have been laid out in the Appendix. The key features described there are necessary if the terminal device is to be used in solving unstructured problems. The device has worked adequately in its three years of operation and it is clear to us that hardware will not be a principal bottleneck. Very few manufacturers currently offer an adequate terminal but this situation is already showing signs of change and it is unlikely that hardware will prove to be a major constraint.

Software

This aspect of a management decision system is among the most difficult. What is required is a software architectural structure that will support an individual with his particular problems and yet be generalizable to other users. Unlike previous MIS support which was functionally oriented, and hence largely independent of changes in users, the MDS software has to support widely different users on widely different applications.

The software developed for this project has subsequently been found adequate for use with other managers in other application areas, so we can claim a degree of generality. However, with such brief experience we are unwilling to make any claims as to the general-purpose nature of this software. It will certainly be more luck than judgment if the system continues to be general enough to carry us through the current expansion plans. Specific points are given on the software in the Appendix.

Systems Design

As with all managerial computer applications it is important to understand the systems design process and the system justification.[1] The design process followed in this case was to build a descriptive model of the previous decision-making process. From this, and from discussions to identify the objectives of the managers involved, analysis was done to identify the information and computational requirements that are theoretically involved in designing a normative model. These two can then be contrasted and the bottlenecks identified. The Management Decision System is then developed to support the process, and in particular to deal with the bottlenecks. The model actually developed, of course, falls short of the normative and yields a third model, the new process. The impact on each stage of the process can be clearly identified and a decision made as to whether the benefits are tangible. If so, then of course the cost/benefit calculation is fairly straightforward. If the benefits are hard to quantify, at least the effects of the system are clearly singled out and the manager, who

---

[1] See Morton (48).

is affected, can then decide if the particular benefit is worth the cost involved.

Thus in this instance it was possible to identify some "hard" savings, such as the sharp reduction in management time involved. It was also possible to look at inventory levels, stock-outs, back orders, discounts granted, price reductions, the level of obsolete inventory at model change-over time, and other hard measures of system performance. The MDS will only affect these slowly over time and it will never be possible to connect use of the system *directly* with improvement in these "hard" variables. However, over time a trend may develop and the managers directly involved can make their own decisions about cause and effect relationships.

One way of assessing the value is to take the approach used in this experiment, that is, model the decision process before and after the introduction of the system and look at the changes. The managers involved can then decide if these changes in the decision process are worth the costs involved. For example, the managers developed several alternative solutions to their problems with the new system, whereas under the old one they stopped at the first acceptable solution. There is no certain way of determining the benefit in improved decision making of having these several alternatives to choose from. It seems intuitively reasonable that with several choices the managers will select the "best" of these on the basis of their experience and that this solution will on average be better than the one and only solution they used to have. There is no way of proving this to be a fact, but by identifying this particular impact the managers were able to ask themselves, is this worth X number of dollars, where X number of dollars is some relevant portion of the total cost. An explicit system evaluation and justification is a necessary part of the implementation process.

Introduction of the MDS System
Implementation—The Experimental Process

From the beginning, this project was centered around the notion that the greatest amount of insight could be gained from examining the use of a visual display system in an ongoing business environment. The use of the system by a line manager who had a complex problem to solve, for which he was responsible, seemed to provide the best environment in which to assess the impact of the system realistically.

The particular problem area chosen is of vital concern to the managers involved. The dollar profits or losses that result from their decisions are large and affect the performance of the division to a noticeable degree. They have to develop a production and marketing plan for the following twelve months. In addition, they set the detailed production levels for the months which are 60 and 90 days in the future. This decision triggers the purchase or manufacture of all components at the 90-day point. They freeze the 60-day forecast at some level, and the detailed production scheduling then takes place at the factory. As was pointed out in Chapters 4 and 5, they must trade off the production constraints with the marketing requirements. They must have the right quantity of product in the system at the right time and in the right place. This should be done at the minimum cost, which means trying for stable production levels and products made in economic lot sizes. The company's market share is about 5% of the total industry, which last year produced 6.5 million units. This implies that the managers are concerned with the strategy of producing $70 to $120 million[2] worth of laundry equipment. Savings of 1% can be significant, as can errors in planning for either production or sales.

A simple indication of the significance of the problem are the time and effort that used to go into trying to solve the task under the old system: One month of elapsed time and from one to three managers involved all month, trying to plan in the best way given the technology then available.

The motivation of the managers was high but, by the same token, their tolerance level for experimenting with devices that were of no help was low. Theirs is a fast-moving area of concern and there are always planning and strategy decisions to be made, to say nothing of the firefighting activities that constantly clamor for attention. Any infringement on their time has to have a high potential payoff in order to obtain their cooperation.

---

[2] Assuming a hypothetical average distributor cost of $200.

There were four major stages in the experimental process, each of which is discussed below:

(1) Initial Observation

The description of the "old" process in Chapters 4 and 5 was derived from a three-month period of intense observation and three further months of spot-checking. In the first three-month period the author was constantly present at all meetings and discussions connected with the problem area. In addition, trips were taken (with the managers concerned) to the factory and major warehouse locations. The three-month follow-up period involved attendance at meetings at the factory and the corporate headquarters where this problem area and these managers were involved.

(2) Implementation

Following the first four months of observation, work was begun on the development of the systems design for this process using the visual display device. None of the possibilities or alternative uses of the device were mentioned seriously to the managers during this phase. A nine-month (elapsed) period of implementation followed during which continuous low-frequency contact was maintained with the managers, and their decision process was kept under observation.

(3) Trials with Test Data

When a minimum working set of the system was functioning and largely debugged, the Market Planning Manager (MPM) and his staff were shown the device and its operation. Test data were used exclusively during this two-month period of teaching and modification. The teaching turned out to be an interesting process. The MPM found no difficulty using the device, and the light-pen/control point combination seemed to be easy to learn and remember. However, the amount of time and effort it would take to make the device completely understandable and entirely natural to use was misjudged. Each individual action with the system was learned easily and rapidly. Combining these into a natural way of arriving at an answer, without any thought, required in-depth understanding of the manager's style of problem-solving. That is, the specific control points were easy to use and each one alone was self-evident after one or two practice tries. To this extent the system exceeded expectations. However, the process of combining the control points to design more complex and mean-ingful patterns of action meant some system changes to reflect the users' habits and styles which had not previously been fully understood.

For example, the notion of the end-point-projection routine (see Appendix C) was quickly understood and used in a simple example. (The sales forecast is changed by + 10,000 units and this quantity is added in during the last five months of the year in proportion to each month's seasonal factor.) The users later wanted a production figure in each month that would give a three-month supply of inventory; they started to change each month one at a time—the notion of using the end-point-projection on the production line did not occur to them. Therefore, another option was built and added to the system. By a series of such changes to the system, plus some corresponding changes in their style of working, they built up a good working relationship with the system.

The other managers had much less difficulty. Probably not more than one hour was spent in teaching. This was partly due to the fact that the MPM acted as instructor in the process of his using the device to arrive at joint answers and, because of his previous relationships, he was an effective instructor. Also, of course, the system had been modified to reflect the group process. The new users were familiar and apparently comfortable after one session of use.

The systems design was further modified to include the reaction of the other managers during the rest of the trial period. Several items that had been omitted from the system, or misunderstood, and hence were incorrect, were changed. These corrections amounted to about two man/months of programming changes.

The trials with the test data took about two months before all of the original system was debugged and the necessary modifications made. After the results reported here were collected, there were continuous modifications, and expansion of the system as its use was tested with other managers and other decisions.

(4) Real Observation

The first time the system was used with "live" data was the period in which the observations were started (see Chapter 7). The data on the previous month's performance were made available from their normal sources, punched and put on the drum. Much of these data were available from the real-time data-base, but in this initial experimental period it was simpler to punch and load.

As the managers used the live data, they required very little in the way of assistance in dealing with the manipulations they wanted. In fact, after the first few sessions they did not need any further help, although they continued to make suggestions for extensions and improvements.

A tape recorder and Polaroid camera were used during the problem-solving process as the media with which to record events. The Polaroid camera turned out to be a simple and inexpensive means of recording the display being examined, while the tape recorder permitted subsequent replays of the conversation and remarks of the managers who had been asked to verbalize the thoughts passing through their minds as they used the system to solve their task.

This protocol was used in two ways. A flow-chart of the new decision-making process was constructed (see Exhibit 7–1), together with some observations on the overall process. In addition, in Chapter 8 there is a detailed discussion of the specific results arranged by the nine cells of the framework discussed in Chapter 3.

The system goals have remained relevant over the life of the project and so can probably be considered a reasonable set. The implementation strategy has stood up in other application areas that we have tried, but there is clearly a lot of work to be done before any claims can be made as to its general use. The further detail contained in Appendix C provides a clearer view of the software structure.

Chapter 7

IMPACT OF THE MDS ON THE DECISION STRUCTURE

THE CONCERN IN THIS CHAPTER is to provide a feel for the way in which the overall structure of the process changed. The manner in which the model of the decision process changed is discussed first, and then the causes for the marked reduction in time of the new process are examined. The detailed cell-by-cell analysis is in Chapter 8 where specific types of impacts can be seen, as well as examples of the system in operation.

In the new system the iteration between Intelligence and Design and Choice is much more rapid. It is a continuous, fast-moving, iterative process where the managers generate a series of successive approximations to their notion of a satisfactory solution.

Each model is started and *processed to completion* through as many of the nine subphases as seem necessary at the time. When all models have been dealt with individually, the entire system (all models) is examined to determine if a satisfactory composite solution has been reached. This process is repeated enough times to reach a satisfactory state.

The considerable shifting from one subphase to another is possible because of the ease of using the system and the resulting short time involved. This series of successive approximations is done fast enough that the users remember what has happened before—that is, they are able to keep up momentum and capitalize on the information "stored" in their own "short-term" memories. This tight, probing investigation and analysis of each subproblem is in marked contrast to the artificial and long-drawn-out analysis that went on before.

In the material that follows, this shift in structure is looked at in two ways. The first is to discuss the model of the new decision process, particularly in contrast with the model of the previous process. The second way of looking at the structural change is to explore a time graph of the old and new processes, so the reasons for the change in time can be understood.

Model of the New Decision Process

There was a marked change in the overall decision-making process. It was collapsed sharply in time and also in structure. Instead of taking six working days in twenty elapsed days, the process took half a working day. Instead of dealing with all models in each of a series of stages, the managers took one model and dealt with it until completion.

Exhibit 7–1 is the flow chart of the old decision-making process. It has the same structure as the one given in the description of this process in Exhibit 4–4. The wording within the boxes has been changed to reflect the terminology discussed in Chapter 5.

In Exhibit 7–1 there are three areas bounded by dotted lines. The process within each of these areas is basically the same, but in each case it is concerned with a different set of variables. More specifically:

Area I.

In this segment the managers developed the sales forecast for the aggregate level. In addition, a very rough production forecast was made.

Area II.

Here sales plans for models were developed and the aggregates reworked if necessary.

Area III.

Production plans by model were generated together with the necessary adjustment to the sales plans.

EXHIBIT 7–1

OLD PROCESS—DECISION-MAKING CYCLE

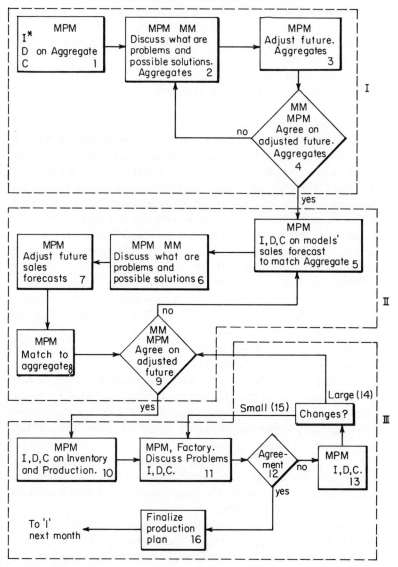

* I, D, C = Intelligence, Design, Choice.

As can be seen from Exhibit 7–1, the structure of these three subareas was basically the same.

The dotted area in Exhibit 7–2, the new process, corresponds to those in Exhibit 7–1. In other words, the structure is the same. However, under the former system, the decision was spread out linearly over time, a simple sequential process. Under the new system it is no longer as linear. The old system considered each of the three phases as a separate process and all models were covered within each phase. In the new process, each model is considered in turn and taken through as many phases as necessary.

The former system was constrained by the limitations of manual processing and the batch computer runs. These constraints largely dictated how the problem had to be attacked. With the new system the technology gives the managers great freedom in organizing themselves to solve the planning problem as they see fit. That is, the former system was arranged to *process the data* as efficiently as possible, given the bottlenecks mentioned in Chapter 4. The new system allows each individual model to be processed through all the steps necessary to arrive at a solution.

The boxes enclosed in the solid lines (boxes 2 and 8) in Exhibit 7–2 are functions that were not performed in the previous system. The managers argued that with the old process they did not have time to have a joint review session. What happened, of course, is that the MPM made the complete review by himself. From his remarks and observation, the final review was cursory at best due to the time pressures involved at the end of the month.

In the new system the managers work from the detail up to the aggregate instead of vice versa. (Appendix D.) In the old process the aggregates (washers, tumblers, agitators) were forecast first and then the models were processed. The two were then reconciled (i.e., the sum of the models was matched with the appropriate aggregate); but as has been noted in Chapter 4, this reconciliation tended to be done in the most convenient fashion, without regard to potential accuracy.

In the new process the managers worked invariably with the models first. They then developed their aggregate, but in reconciling they tended to attach more importance to the detailed forecasts (see Appendix D). The significance of this is that attaching

EXHIBIT 7–2

NEW PROCESS—DECISION-MAKING CYCLE*

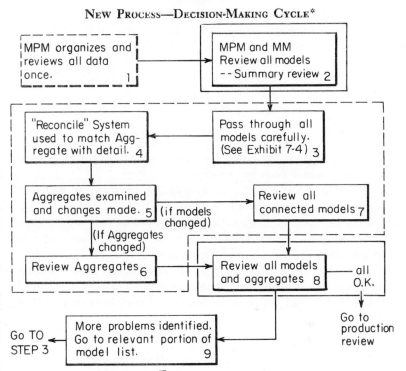

* See Notes for explanation.

NOTES: (Comments are keyed to box)

1. This process was employed by the MPM in sessions 1 and 2 but not thereafter. The manager indicated (see Appendix D) after the third session that he would no longer do this. Box 2 now became the first step.

2. No models are changed. This is a once-over-lightly review to find potential problems.

3. Each of the models is taken in turn and examined.

4. When the last model is finished, all models are compared with the relevant aggregate. No changes are made until step 7 is finished.

5. Step 3 repeated for aggregate.

6. 7. Depending on results of steps 4 and 5 one or both of the aggregates and various models are changed.

8. Models are then reviewed as in step 2.

9. If any problems are seen from step 8, then the process is iterated from step 3.

too much importance to the aggregate can lead to errors. The whole is only the sum of the parts, and it is the *parts* that are under the managers' control. If a certain forecast is made for agitators (aggregate), it can only be achieved by selling specific models. It is these models that are under control of the division. It is reasonable to consider most closely those variables that are under managerial control.

Under the new system the structure of the decision-making process is not distorted by the requirements of the data-manipulation process. Hence, the managers can focus on the variables under their control and deal with them in a way that fits naturally with their own problem-solving methods.

The managers were able to solve the problem in the way that seemed best to them and the technology gave them complete freedom to call on any computation or models they felt were useful. They could call for the data in any sequence or format that was appropriate to the specifics of the problem at hand. With this sort of flexibility and problem-solving power it would seem possible to generate more satisfactory solutions. The managers involved felt that they had better understanding of the situation and that their planning was more effective.

Changes in the Decision-Making Core

There is a sharp contrast in the decision-making core of the two processes. Decision-making core refers here to that part of the process where the managers were dealing with one *specific* subproblem as opposed to the complete planning process for all models. For example, has model X-1 performed as well as it should have? Before the MDS was used, the separate physical sessions would be concerned with some partial *segment* of the nine-celled process. For example, all models would be contrasted to their objective in one session and a few picked for closer examination. Rough suggestions were made for improving the problem models. The meeting would adjourn and the suggestions would be worked on by the staff, and new spread sheets developed. Then another session would be convened to examine the design possibilities such as an increase in advertising or a shift in timing of production runs. This issue would be examined across all models, suggestions made, and a further adjournment for more processing. These separate sessions made it hard for the managers to follow one strategy through to completion.

Following the introduction of the MDS there was a much tighter decision process. A strategy for *one model* was picked up and taken through to its logical conclusion: that is, through the intelligence, design and choice phases with complete freedom to move among the phases.

Exhibits 7–3 and 7–4 with their related notes portray this change in summary form. Exhibit 7–3 is characterized by the clear separation of the major phases, these often occurring in different meetings at different points in time. In contrast, Exhibit 7–4 shows all of the phases occurring in one session.

A feature of the process which is clearly discernible from the protocol (see Appendix D) but not easily portrayed in Exhibit 7–4 is the degree to which the managers moved back and forth between the boxes in Exhibit 7–4. They cycled often and rapidly through both the three major phases as well as the nine subphases. This flexibility allowed them to follow their train of thought through to an answer which they could evaluate. It provided them with the power to take an idea and follow it immediately through to its logical conclusion.

In summary, the difference in the decision-making core before and after the MDS is one of structure. Before the MDS the process was constrained by the managers' ability to manipulate data. Therefore, it was a serial process with a few feedback loops. In addition, the managers used one set of manipulations for all models instead of taking one model and processing it through all the manipulations required to arrive at a final solution. The structure resulting after the MDS is one that matches management's notion of natural problem solving—it was flexible enough to match what the managers wanted to do.

Time-Graph of the New Decision Process

The most noticeable impact of the new system, of course, is time. The very much greater speed with which the job can be

EXHIBIT 7–3

Former Decision Process*

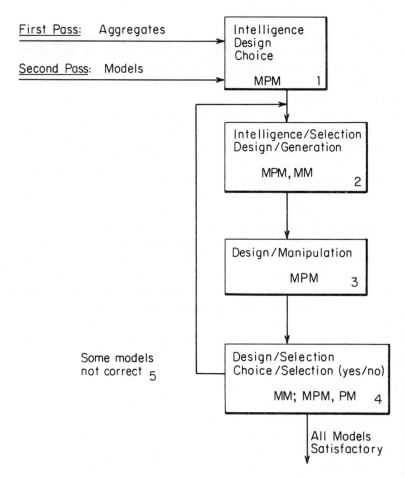

* Each box is a separate session. The time between boxes is not less than one-half day.

Notes: (Numbers correspond to the number on the flow chart, Exhibit 7–3.)
1. The MPM and staff, went through the generation, manipulation, and selection process with the information at hand and came up with the initial version of the solution.

done affects both the overall process and the decision-making core. Exhibit 7–5 summarizes the time differences between the three sets of trials of the new process and the old process.

The most dramatic time shifts occur when there is manipulation involved. Even here the figures are understated because under the new process there is a great deal more manipulation carried out, in a fraction of the former time.

The difference between elapsed time and working time in the old process was due largely to the difficulty of scheduling meetings between the parties involved. The managers had traveling to do, particularly the MM, so that arranging the next meeting tended to pose some kind of scheduling problem.

This shift in the time involved is not considered to be particularly significant in and of itself. The direct cost savings are not dramatic, and this time-saving has real benefit only if the managers use the time thus released in some meaningful way. Obviously, the opportunities for using the time to improve the planning and control process could result in very high payoff. This is discussed in more detail in Chapter 8.

The major impact of the reduction in time is found in the changes to the style and structure of the decision process, the two points discussed earlier in this chapter.

---

2. The MPM and the MM then met to discuss jointly the "first approximation" solution. Direction of changes and rough magnitudes were agreed on.

3. The MPM and staff worked with suggestions from 2 to come up with the second approximation.

4. The MPM and MM looked at results of 3 and selected those that were satisfactory. Similarly the PM and MPM evaluated the results. For those that were not satisfactory, a different approach was agreed to and left for step 3.

5. This process of 4, 2, 3 was cycled until all were satisfactory.

6. The entire sequence (1–5) was cycled again at the model level.

This process was characterized by the clear separation of the Intelligence, Design, and Choice phases and subphases. They occurred in different meetings at different points in time.

EXHIBIT 7–4

Decision Process with the MDS*

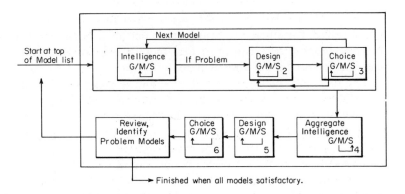

→ Finished when all models satisfactory.

* This is one session with no break. Small arrows with the G/M/S (Generation/Manipulation/Selection) indicate cycling through these subphases several times.

NOTES: (Numbers correspond to the number in the boxes, Exhibit 7–4.)

1. The managers would look at the graph for a model, add or remove information and decide if the model was a problem (see Exhibit 7–2). If not, they might select further manipulation and then end up deciding the model was satisfactory, or else they might go through the design process again.

2. In the design stage, still with the same model as in 1 above, they would execute the solution they had thought of, look at the impact on the screen and either (a) select it as a possible solution, passing on to 3, or (b) try some other approach (i.e., back to generation).

3. Choice was always made between the previous solution and the current solution—the two latest ones in the managers' minds. Again iteration took place if it was an unappealing solution to the managers.

4, 5, 6. With all the models processed, the aggregates were cycled through in the same fashion (as 1, 2, 3 above) and then possibly the models once again (see Exhibit 7–3).

7. The overall status at the end of this first approximation was evaluated by reviewing all models. A subset of problem models was passed through the entire process again.

Note that this process has the Intelligence, Design, and Choice phases in one session.

EXHIBIT 7-5

TIME COMPARISONS, OLD AND NEW PROCESS

New Process Exhibit 7-2 **	Old Process Exhibit 7-1	Observation Sessions (minutes) *			Old Process (minutes)	Activity
		Group 1	Group 2	Group 3		
1	† 1	40	—	—	500	Organize and review data.
2	—	—	20	15	—	Summary review of all models, did not take place in Session 1.
3	5, 6, 7, 10, 11, 12	110	90	130	1,000	Pass through models, identify problems and test solutions.
4	8, 10	30	20	15		Reconcile differences, develop consistent plan.
5	3, 4, 8	5	15	15	300	Aggregate forecast examined and modified. This box was entered several times in Sessions 2 and 3.
6	3, 4	10	15	30	60	Review process on aggregates and models was cycled several times and used by the managers to gain perspective.
7	5, 6	10	35	45	700	Used in the six-month period covered by Groups 2 and 3 to look into future periods to see where trends were leading.
8	2, 3, 6, 7					
			½ day		6 days	Total working time. Previous elapsed time 20 days.

* Groups 1, 2, 3 are each an average of three one-month periods. Data have been rounded to the nearest significant digit. For example, Group 1 is an average of April, May, June.

** Numbers refer to boxes in Exhibit 7-1.

† Numbers refer to boxes in Exhibit 7-2.

Chapter 8

DETAILED IMPACT OF THE MANAGEMENT DECISION SYSTEM

IN GENERAL, EXPECTATIONS AS TO THE LIKELY IMPACTS of the MDS were confirmed. The impact differed in detail from that which was expected, but the general characteristics were similar: the system had an impact on the bottlenecks which had been experienced under the old system. Chapter 1 made some general observations as to the impact of the MDS on the decision-making process. These were derived from the detailed examination of the decision process (a summary is included in this chapter). Chapter 9 contains a broader discussion of the conclusions, plus some comment on the implications of this approach for management.

The five major points that were made earlier on the overall impact were as follows:

Operational Use

The system was able to be used as an operational tool. Line and staff managers with no technical background were able to use the system effectively.

Impact on Time

Response time by the system to a request or a suggestion by the managers was reduced to seconds. This was consistent with the managers' normal mental problem-solving activity. Hence data and computation did not interfere with their problem-solving process. This lack of interference in turn led to a reduction in elapsed time, although the age, or currency, of the data-base was unchanged from previous manual methods.

Problem Finding

The ability to request and structure data at will, as well as the graphical features of the system permitted the managers to find potential or existing problems rapidly and effectively.

Problem Solving

By having access to the key variables in a relevant form and being able to make changes readily and quickly the managers developed several solutions to any given problem. In addition, their solutions were based on a clear view of the facts since the contents of data-base, the manipulative power of the models, and the presentation capacity of the system were all available.

Communications Role of the MDS

The system proved to be an effective means of communication between the managers. Grouped around the system they were able to explain points to each other and reduce the "noise" level of their communications.

Lying behind these points is the analysis of the protocol and other evidence from the nine months of heavy experimentation. A summary of this analysis follows below. It is arranged by the nine cells of the framework developed in Chapter 3. Extracts from the protocol of the decision makers and other material is given in Appendix D.

Detailed Impact by Cell

This section contains summary comments on the impacts that were expected, in relation to those that actually occurred. As noted in Chapter 5, the potential impact of the MDS was indicated at the end of the discussion of each cell. These observations are discussed briefly here to provide some overview of the impact; further detail is in Appendix D which includes a summary of the observations and protocol for each of the cells.

At the beginning of each of the nine cells, the projections given in Chapter 5 are repeated.

Cell 1. Intelligence/Generation

The MDS was not expected to have any significant impact on this phase of the decision-making process.[1]

Since the MDS used exactly the same data as the old process, there was no impact. The information content of this data was radically altered by the MDS through the use of graphs, but this is taken into account in the remaining cells.

Cell 2. Intelligence/Manipulation

(1) Cut the time for manipulation to such an extent that other interested persons will take part in the search process.

The implication (developed in Chapter 5), for this expected impact was that the MM and the PM would be involved in some portion of the search for problems. In actual fact the MM and PM became involved for the entire process. They were active participants in the intelligence phase.

(2) Increase the number and types of manipulations used.

The protocol and observations indicate that there was a change in the type and quantity of the manipulation. The managers made explicit comparisons between the variables (as noted in D, B–2–b).[2] These variables were:

Sales: objective, actual, forecast, planned.
Production: forecast, planned.
Inventory: actual, objective.

---

[1] From Chapter 5.

[2] D, B–2–b refers to Appendix D, Detailed Observations, Cell 2, item b. This notation is used throughout this chapter.

The former process involved the MPM alone, looking at whichever variables seemed reasonable, and the later sessions with the MM and the PM involved little or no manipulation in this phase, as the problems were largely identified by an informal intuitive process. With the new system each manager called for data on the screen to support his search and problem identification process.

(3) Allow greater flexibility in the values used for the parameters in any one manipulation.

In the former process the only manipulation was to copy numbers on the spread sheets. In the present process they use the manipulation noted in D, B–2. The managers did change specific values in different months and looked at the resulting pattern, a sequence such as asking for 3 months' supply of inventory in all months and then looking at the new production requirements. At no stage did management ask for a more flexible system during the Intelligence phases, so it is reasonable to assume that the MDS was flexible enough for currently perceived needs.

(4) Increase the investigation of patterns of performance identified by any member involved as being atypical.
(5) Result in change in the problem "search" process, a change toward greater depth of search.

The protocol in D, B–2, D, B–3 and D, B–4 supports these points. Depth of analysis is implied in the consistent and complete method of search used in the intelligence phase. As indicated in D, B–2–b and D, B–3–c all of the models were reviewed in turn. As each model appeared on the screen, it would be discussed and some manipulation would result from this. The managers found it useful to be present, together, through the whole process. The interaction between them, with each making his point through the MDS, led to discussion on each and every model.

To the extent this discussion, which did not exist before, was useful and led to greater understanding of the situation, then the problem "search" process was conducted with greater depth.

Cell 3. Intelligence/Selection

(1) Reduce the time spent in meetings concerned with the "intelligence" phase.

The time reduction was dramatic and gave rise to many of the other effects discussed in this section. The MDS reduced the time spent on all aspects of the problem from 6 days to ½ day and on this particular phase by a factor of 10:1.

(2) Examine those items selected for investigation more thoroughly than before. This would involve more displays of several combinations of variables; essentially, iteration through Phases 2 and 3.

The significant impact here is due to the reduction in time between the formulation of a "what if" question and the response. For example, a typical question was, ". . . What if we cut production of this model by 50% in August . . . how will our availability (inventory, month's supply) look . . . ?" The immediate response possible to this type of question led to a different form of problem solving. The interaction that the MDS allowed led to the managers' asking one or more questions for each model. To the extent these questions were useful, then their exploration of the models was more thorough than before.

(3) Make it possible for the MM, who knows the marketplace best, to take part in the problem search process.

In the experiment the MM not only took part in the intelligence phase, he also actively participated in the Design and Choice phases. The reduction in time and the ease of interaction were the two reasons he quoted for this. He found the MDS useful in analysis as well as faster.

(4) Provide "information" from the display more readily than from the previous process.

Evidence for this point is in D, B–3–c where the managers' comments and the short time between their actions with the light-pen indicated that they had read some message from the information in the display and were acting on it.

From the managers' comments on the ease of understanding the information portrayed, it can be concluded that graphical information can be more readily understood than tabular data. The comments and performance indicated that, for these managers at least, the information content in graphical data was considerably higher than with the familiar tabular format.

Cell 4. Design/Generation

(1) Subphases 2 and 3 would involve a great many more manipulations and comparisons than the old process.

The protocol (D, B–2 and D, B–3) indicates that there was considerably more manipulation with the MDS, particularly in the subphases of Intelligence/Manipulation and Intelligence/Selection.

(2) Subphase 4, 5, and 6 would be cycled through several times for each identified problem in an attempt to design a more adequate solution.

This impact is substantiated by the points made in D, B–4–a. The managers would arrive at a solution for a model, admit it looked satisfactory, but then go on to try another modification. The table in D, B–4–a indicates the extent to which this occurred. In addition, after the second set of sessions, the managers made the point that they were able to try out different solutions.

The reasons for this, again, are the ease and speed of interaction. Because the managers were able to implement a solution and see the results in a short enough time period, they made use of this facility.

(3) The managers involved would participate in the design phase together.

This was pointed out, above, as having occurred. The impact is particularly noticeable, from the protocol, in the design phase. New solutions, which were suggested by the managers, not the MDS, came from all of the managers. From the protocol it appears that this interaction between the managers is quite possibly more creative and beneficial than with any of them operating alone. The MDS has only an indirect effect here, that is, it shortened the time and improved the interaction so the managers were willing to sit through the whole process. Because they were together, the Design/Generation phase appears to have benefited. The MDS itself did not suggest an answer. There were no predictive models involved in this early stage.

Cell 5. Design/Manipulation

(1) Allow a greater number of "solutions" to be tested out, that is, solutions involving different variables.

The point was substantiated by the managers' performance with the MDS. D, B–2–b and D, B–5–a indicate the different kinds of variables used. For example, they might change specific months in the production plan one time, alter the sales plans (and hence merchandising effort) another time, and perhaps use a fixed month's supply a third time. These and other variations were all used during the problem-solving process.

Section D, B–5–b makes the point that the increase in manipulation was significant. The absolute level is such that it would be completely unrealistic to plan to do such manipulation in any other fashion. To do this manually would be too long and expensive and a batch computer would be too slow in response.

(2) Allow several different values for the same variable to be tested.

Changing the same variable, using a different value for the same month, was done as frequently as changing the variable itself. That is, the managers might try another solution, such as altering production instead of sales, or they might try a different value in their sales plan. Neither alternative predominated and the managers suggested both types of solution.

Cell 6. Design/Selection

(1) Several modifications would be tried with each initial "solution."

Not a single solution (D, B–6–b) was generated, implemented, and chosen with only one pass. Each initial solution invariably had at least one modification before acceptance. This experimentation with solutions was often limited (D, B–7–a) when the model had only a simple problem. With larger problems the design phase was cycled from two to eight times. This experimentation with the solution could well have a favorable effect on the quality of the final answer.

(2) More than one satisfactory solution would be generated and held over for the next phase.

The protocol shows that this took place (D, B–6–a) but not in the fashion expected when this impact was discussed in Chapter 5. The managers never generated more than two solutions at any one time. The selection phase was never entered with more than two solutions.

The reasons for not developing a list of three or four possible solutions seem to have been due to the limited memory power of the human being and the initial inflexibility of the MDS. The MDS was not set up to facilitate recall of a solution. There is no inherent difficulty in doing this but the capability was not provided in the initial system software.

(3) The managers would develop a more explicit set of criteria as to what constitutes an acceptable solution.

This projected impact of the MDS did not materialize during the initial study. There was no indication that the managers were more aware of the cause and effect relationships in their problems. However, it may have been unreasonable to expect such "insight" to come so soon. There is evidence, discussed in Chapter 9, to indicate that this began to happen in the later stages of development.

Cell 7. Choice/Generation

(1) The managers would repeat the design phase more than once.

The section 6–2, above, points out that there were several solutions generated and that this involved cycling through the 4, 5 and 6 stages several times. The re-entry into the design process was initiated by the managers at different points in the process. The protocol D, B–7 provides an example of this.

(2) The managers would generate several alternative solutions.

The protocol D, B–7 provides some indication of the extent to which the managers did generate alternative solutions. They dealt with these in a sequential fashion since they were only comparing two at a time and sometimes made four sets of comparisons. However, they did generate alternatives in a systematic way for all the significant problems that they identified. This is in marked contrast to the process discussed in Chapter 4, where the first acceptable solution was used.

Cell 8. Choice/Manipulation

The MDS was not expected to have much impact on this cell.

This turned out to be partly true, but the reasons were not as described in Chapter 5. The managers used the MDS on a few occasions to redisplay the previous solution. This process was so awkward, given the current implementation of the MDS software, that it was not used more than three times. Instead, the managers relied upon their memory to make the comparison with the previous solution.

What happens when the MDS is designed to handle this function adequately is discussed in Chapter 9.

Cell 9. Choice/Selection

The MDS was not expected to have any significant impact in this phase.

The observations in D, B–9–a and D, B–9–b show that this was not, in fact, what happened. The MDS had two kinds of impact on this phase. The first impact was due to the speed of interaction. Since this was rapid, the managers moved easily and naturally from the design to choice phases, and back again. The decision-making process was no longer as neatly compartmentalized. This seemed to encourage experimentation; at least the managers had two acceptable alternatives in front of them and yet in 25% of the cases, they tried at least a third alternative. In this respect, the Choice/Selection phase was affected by the MDS.

The second impact is a function of having the managers present, together with the system, in this phase. Discussion of the solution on the MDS tube-face would lead them to experiment and, essentially, move back to Phase 4 or 7 and come up with another solution. This phase changed from being an automatic selection of the single alternative to being an opportunity for creative selection of a developing alternative.

CONCLUSIONS

The MDS had a significant impact on the decision-making process. The immediate and clearly identifiable impacts have been summarized above. These indicate that by and large the project expectations were fulfilled, and that the managers found the system of considerable benefit to this unstructured problem. It is interesting to note that the impact on the decision process came from the ability to see the relevant information organized in a consistent way, from the access to manipulative power, and from the improved communication. The display terminal is merely a tool to provide this and has no intrinsic merit in and of itself. There are some other interesting issues that were raised in the course of this experiment, and Chapter 9 is devoted to these more speculative questions.

Chapter 9

Overview of Experimental Findings

THE PREVIOUS CHAPTERS THAT DISCUSS THE BACKGROUND of the project and its outcome should have established the point that what we have chosen to call a Management Decision System is not merely a collection of hardware and software. Rather, it is a point of view made operationally feasible by changes in technology. In this respect it is argued that the scarcest resource is talented management time, and that this should be maximized wherever possible.

One way of maximizing the use of management time is to develop an MDS to support the manager. As indicated in the preceding material this development has two major components: first, the analysis to determine what the critical decisions are and the best way of making them, and second, the development of a system that couples the manager to the models, data-base, and computational power of the MDS. These two components of the Management Decision Systems approach must go together. Failure to do a decent job of analysis may result in solving the wrong problem or designing an inappropriate system for problem solution. Merely analyzing a problem does not bring about as much change as is possible in the effectiveness of managers' decisions.

Traditional Management Information Systems have typically focused on generating data and reports for the functional aspects of a business. Such streams of computer-based functional data, often for structured problems (for example, production control and financial accounting activity), are designed to support the day-to-day operations of the firm. Rarely are they deliberately designed to support significant *managerial* decisions. A Management Decision System approach suggests that there are ways to support certain classes of management decision making and that there are some key analytical steps to be taken before a particular MDS is actually designed and built.

This analysis process is similar to an analysis of problems in any field and bears a direct relationship to the problem of systems analysis in the traditional MIS field. Unlike the traditional MIS area the analysis cannot be done by systems analysts or technicians alone. In deciding what is a critical decision and identifying the key variables, the manager himself must be involved. A system is being built to support his decisions; hence, there is no alternative in a practical setting to his getting heavily involved. He has the "feel" for the management issues, so he has to take a major role in determining what is relevant for the new system.

Generalizing from the sequence of steps that occurred in Chapters 3 to 8 it is apparent that there ought to be at least the following stages in the analysis process:

Definition and classification of objectives. Given an organizational unit there is almost always a need to define sharply and in operational terms the goals and objectives involved. This definition allows the analysis to take place for a relevant problem with the relevant managers. There are, of course, hierarchies of such objectives, and the lowest level relevant to the MDS process is that which identifies the objectives for the decision being examined.

Description of the current decision process. Having a clear notion of the objectives of the decision it then becomes necessary to have a thorough, descriptive model of the current decision process. This involves the kinds of data used, the kinds of manipulation that take place, and the whole sequence of the decision process.

After the model has been established, the objectives can often be further clarified and restated in a more operational fashion.

Definition of a normative model of the decision-making process.
What is an ideal way of achieving the objectives? Which data
should be looked at, what models should be used, and what are the
criteria involved?

Comparison of these two models: the normative with the actual.
The design criteria for the new system should become clear, as
soon as the comparison has been made. To be successful, the new
design must move the decision process substantially toward the normative model. For certain problems a computer-driven terminal
system will be appropriate, in other cases this analysis will show
that some other approach is more effective.

*Building a descriptive model of the manager's decision process,
using the new system.* After implementation, this further stage of
modeling the new decision process is important. By comparing this
with the original descriptive model it is possible to see the changes
that have taken place. This analysis can then form the basis of a
cost/benefit study.

This five-step analysis in the MDS approach is not only necessary but essential. The result, in cases where an MDS is appropriate, is a decent design that couples the manager with the models,
data-base, and computation that he needs to solve his problem
effectively.

Given these five steps as background to the use of an MDS,
the comments that follow represent an overview of the impact of
the experiment.

SPECIFIC IMPACTS

Interactive terminals, supported by an MDS, are feasible tools
for managers to use on unstructured problems. The technology
and cost situation are such that an MDS is economically viable for
certain classes of unstructured problems. Managers with varied
backgrounds and line responsibilities can find the MDS a useful
tool for some of their problem-solving tasks in areas where the
problems are hard to define explicitly and where solutions involve
complex strategies.

This does not imply, of course, that an MDS is useful for all classes of problems in all environments. In this experiment the *problem* had:

A significant impact, over the year, on the profitability of the organization. This problem was one of the key decisions that was made in the operation of the division.

A large data-base, that is, larger than the managers could conveniently deal with on a manual basis.

A significant amount of manipulation. The data had to be processed through a set of filters to provide signals that had some meaning to the managers.

Several dimensions. There was no one criterion that could be used to identify what was a significant problem, or what was a good solution to a problem.

A need to combine the functional skills of several managers to solve one problem.

Significant complexity to make it extremely difficult to identify cause and effect relationships among the several variables involved. These decisions, therefore, involved the exercise of considerable managerial judgment.

An environment that changed rapidly enough for an analysis to be made on a monthly basis if the company was to respond to market pressures. It was not an environment requiring real-time data, but it was very far from being static.

The results of this experiment seem to indicate that for problems having these general characteristics, a Management Decision System is an operationally useful approach for providing support to line managers in their decision process. This statement is to be carefully distinguished from assertions concerning the utility of graphic terminals in general. Such systems can best be evaluated in a problem context as they only take on value in terms of the impact they have on the effectiveness of a manager.

For example, providing instant access through a visual terminal to traditional accounting data is unlikely to be of value to a line manager, although under some conditions it might be useful in the controller's department. Such an experiment conducted with a line manager would probably result in his not using the system, and the conclusion might then be drawn that visual display terminals are of no use to managers. In fact, in such a setting these terminals are providing him with an ability to reach data for which he has no need, and a reasonable evaluation cannot be made. Careful systems design on a relevant problem is necessary if an MDS is to be useful.

If an MDS is used on a meaningful problem then it can have the impacts discussed in Chapter 8. That is, it can (1) reduce both the elapsed and decision-making time, (2) improve the effectiveness and efficiency of the problem-finding activity, (3) change the problem-solving activities to result in the provision of more alternatives, and (4) change the quality of the communications between managers.

The four points discussed below are in a different category from those discussed in Chapter 8, where some experimental evidence was gained under reasonably controlled conditions. Later usage showed indications of changes in categories other than those discussed in Chapter 8. Four of the most interesting of these tentative impacts are discussed below.

Time Horizons

Time is awkward in many planning situations. The longer the time span, the less precise the information and the more the number of variables that have to be considered. In six months many of the variables that were fixed become variable, and planning becomes that much more complex. There is, therefore, a natural tendency to avoid ambiguity and complexity and stay with short planning horizons, despite the very obvious danger of not seeing shifts in the environment rapidly enough to have the organization adapt at least cost.

In this experiment, under the old process, the managers concentrated the bulk of their attention on the four-month period immediately ahead. In the early part of the calendar year they would look ahead on occasion, but most of their attention was focused on the shorter term. Their task was further complicated by the use of a calendar and fiscal year that was six months out of phase from the model year. That is, objectives and plans were made on a January to December fiscal year, but new models were generally introduced annually in June. This led to difficulties in meshing with plans that were on the other time frame, and there was a natural tendency to think in terms of one time span only.

In the new process with the MDS, the managers did make changes in their plans for all future months. In the old process, changes were made in the final two quarters but almost all the attention was given to the periods that were two, three, and four months away. With the MDS, changes were made, and discussions held, in all the months in the 12-month rolling horizon. In this sense, the managers' planning horizons shifted to include more of the longer term. After using the MDS for a while, one would expect that the longer planning horizon would result in fewer crises and a more stable operation. Obviously the system will have to be used for a long time before this can be tested in any way.

Organization Structure

The communications impact of the MDS is sufficiently strong that it could well provide the impetus for organizational changes. To the extent that a manager is involved in a decision-making process in a role of arbitrator or coordinator, then his role could shift. With the use of the MDS the continuity provided by a coordinator is not required. For example, the time for the decision process was cut sharply enough so that all the managers could be present all of the time. Similarly, the coordinator might not have to concern himself with the supervision of staff work since the computer system could handle a fair amount of the manipulation and presentation of the information.

The arbitration or mediation role that some managers are forced to take in certain decision processes can be time-consuming and unproductive. This was proved in the process discussed in this experiment. In addition, if the problem is not clearly delineated, there can be a considerable amount of unproductive discussion, nominally focused on different strategies for solution, but in practice being used to clarify the issues. The MDS can be used to clarify the issues, directly and unambiguously, and the discussion can focus on the pros and cons of the solution.

To the extent that the organization and its subcomponents have been structured to include people in a decision process to arbitrate or act as coordinator, it seems fairly clear that their roles might usefully change. The managers directly involved can take over more of the problem-finding and problem-solving activities with the aid of an approach such as the MDS.

Presentation of Information

The managers' response to the cumulative graphical displays was very favorable. They had not used them before, but understood the information content quickly and found that this graphical portrayal of relational information was useful.

The graphs had the effect of condensing the data volume very sharply and at the same time provided the user with some context. From one graph the user could work with trends and patterns in approximately seven or eight different data sets without any apparent difficulty. The amount of information that can usefully be presented in one display is a function of several variables, including the application, the manager, the form of presentation, and so forth. It is clear that much more work will have to be done before enough has been learned to make really effective use of the powers inherent in such displays. The impact is there, but not enough is known yet about why it occurred.

All of the managers' responses indicate that the presentation of the information was a significant feature of the MDS. In addition, it appears that these managers had no trouble remembering patterns, perceiving trends, and interpreting the graphs. All of these were done rapidly, with little learning and to the evident satisfaction of the managers involved.

In other decision situations other forms of presentation would doubtless be useful. The flexibility exists with the MDS to present whatever mix and style of display that is relevant and effective in the situation.

Planning

The length of the decision cycle is dramatically reduced with the use of the MDS. Therefore, the manager has time previously unavailable to him; in addition, he has his data readily accessible on the MDS. The available data can be searched in greater depth for problems, or the manager can look further ahead in time and try to identify possible problems before they develop. In either case he is likely to be improving his planning process.

There is a further important possibility open to the manager. The system can obviously provide access to models as well as data. With the managers' involvement, simulation models can be built to project forward whatever plans or strategies he has. With the released time he can turn his attention to the areas in which he can use predictive or analytical models and take an active part with the management systems or management science staff in developing them.

The MDS provides an opportunity, both in the time made available and in the more useful technology, for the manager to restructure the whole planning process. He can concern himself with new types of analysis, new information sources, and new ways of planning for the future.

These sorts of activities have occurred to some extent in this particular situation. It is clear that these changes did not occur just because of the MDS. Certainly the system opened up new possibilities and aroused the interest of those concerned but it was coupled with a general concern with the process that is inevitable in any experimental situation. The longer-term implications of this are raised in Chapter 10, but the short-run interest and introspection by the managers clearly occurred in the planning for the decision process.

MANAGEMENT DECISION SYSTEM REQUIREMENTS

Having raised these more speculative issues, this chapter concludes with an overview of the system requirements involved if an organization is to construct an MDS. Implicit in the points made below is the overriding necessity of having serious top management involvement and the full-time attention of a technically qualified individual who also has management breadth and experience. The managers involved in the decision, those for whom the system is being built, have to be actively involved in design, evaluation, and evolution. However, they do need to be guided, cajoled, and helped through this critical process. To do this well requires a systems analyst with managerial experience to be involved with them throughout the process. Given these preconditions the following comments can be made on the basis of this experiment.

Chapter 2 discussed the five components involved in a management decision system. Those were: (1) the manager and problem area, (2) the terminal device, (3) the central computer, (4) the software to support the decision process, and (5) the data-base necessary for the decision. Of these the software is the most ambiguous as it implies a systems design process for the problem area. This in turn requires the manager's time and effort in formulating specifications as the system is being built for him. There is a minimum threshold level of performance that has to exist in each of the five areas if the system is to be effective. However, it is also clear, with the experience gained from this project, that it is not necessary to have all five components developed to an equally advanced stage. One or more of the components can be jury-rigged to get the system up and running as part of a pilot process. From the insights and experience gained in this way, the company's efforts can be allocated much more effectively.

The strategy proposed here implies an incremental approach to the use of an MDS. With a new field such as this it is both expensive and time-consuming to attempt any large-scale cut-over to such a new system. On the other hand, waiting until current applications have generated a complete data-base, or until fully on-line systems are installed, are not normally valid reasons for inaction. The acceptable threshold levels in these five areas can be quite low if an appropriate application area is selected, because the experience gained in design, implementation, and use is invaluable to further effective use of such systems. Some comments on each of these five areas are given in the following material.

Manager and Problem Area

This experiment suggests that the implementation strategy should be to identify different classes of decision process, and then go through a thorough systems analysis effort to build some notions of exactly where and under what conditions various forms of decision support might be useful. This approach involves two critical steps. The first of these is the identification of a significant decision area. Clearly the provision of an interactive terminal to a manager to help him solve some trivial problem, more usually done by an assistant, is not likely to make adequate use of the power of such a terminal in a management setting.

Similarly, to take an existing decision process and convert it, as is, to an interactive terminal system is most unlikely to make full use of the power inherent in the display technology. A careful systems analysis is required to identify the support needs, and if a terminal is required that it is used to best effect in the decision process. This point might be clarified by drawing an analogy with batch computer operations. It is universally recognized that one does not take the old manual, clerical, processing methods and put them on a computer. One goes through a careful systems analysis and design process first, and then converts to the computer. Similarly one does not automatically convert the current decision process to a terminal system without careful analysis.

The manager does not have to have any detailed knowledge of computers. None of those involved in this project had had any computer experience and they did not seem to find this a handicap. To make effective use of the MDS the manager should be competent and have a thorough understanding of the general problem with which he is dealing. It is his "insight" into the problem area which the MDS can best complement.

Assuming that the systems design supports the manager in a way he finds comfortable, then he can have flexible access to a model-bank, data-base, and computational power. These capabilities, coupled with the immediate response (*not* currency) of the system, can provide a manager working on certain classes of unstructured problems with powerful support in his decision process.

The manager can deal with the strategy issues and all judgmental questions, and in addition perhaps maintain and develop his criteria for problem identification and choice of problem solution. The system can take care of the data manipulation and presentation of information, as well as information retrieval. These are functions in which the MDS has a relative advantage over the human being.

With this process of implementation, and careful identification of the role of the terminal and focus on a management problem with the characteristics discussed in Chapter 3, there is every possibility of developing a useful system.

Software

Interactive display terminals are simply mechanical tools. Like all other components of a computer system they take on utility only when they are driven by instructions, for instance, programs that are designed to achieve some purpose. In all of this experimental discussion, reference has been made to the Management Decision System, not to a display device. What is being evaluated is a combination of software and hardware, the program and the terminal. Clearly both are necessary; the terminal features of speed, graphs, and light-pen for interaction cannot now be provided in any other way except by a terminal. These features are employed by the software to provide a powerful and useful tool to the manager.

One could, for example, have an interesting relevant problem and yet be doing a poor job on the software and therefore not have a tool that the manager finds useful. Good software is possible only if the problem has been analyzed with enough insight to understand what support the manager needs. This support may consist of formal models, relevant computation, access to data, graphical presentation, or any combination of these features. Regardless of the set of functions required for the decision process, the software has to be built to be appropriate for the managers and problems involved. The managers have to be able to solve problems the way they like to work, and in a context with which they are familiar.

If this system performance can be obtained only by using expensive analysts and reprogramming for each application, then the costs could well be too high. In the work that has been done since the experiment, the MDS has been tested with other managers in other environments. Working prototype systems have been developed in these areas, and it appears that the basic software architecture is adaptable to new users in new areas. This is partially accomplished by writing the operating system in a higher level language, COBOL, which reduces the cost of modification. It also turns out that the basic kinds of displays and actions used by the managers have many common elements and that new users require reasonably little effort to make these operational.

The systems effort involved in analyzing[1] the managers' decision process and designing software to support it, is large. Not enough has yet been learned to predict how much generality can be built into the software. The software architecture developed for the MDS in other decision environments has been tested and found to hold rather well. However, more use in these other areas will be required before it can be asserted that the system structure is indeed general. Experience with this project indicates that the software and systems problems are of the same order of magnitude as the effort involved with more traditional MIS efforts, such as a new budgeting system or a new inventory control system. That is, large and complex, but one that is well within the abilities of most management systems groups in large firms or consulting companies.

Working with the manager on the problem analysis and systems design phase gets him easily and quickly involved as an active partner in the design. The system after all is for *his* personal use and this makes it simple to get significant managerial involvement. This is quite different from trying to get support from users of, say, a proposed new budget system. That is often perceived as being remote and required by the company but not necessarily of any direct use for each manager. The experience with the MDS was quite different. Once an initial working system was available the users not only were active in the design of their system but continued over time to suggest improvements and additions. They really began to think about improvements that might be made in

---

[1] See Morton (48).

their decision process. This has exciting possibilities for the future and the development of "intelligent" systems as discussed in Chapter 10.

Terminal System

Experience with this project indicates quite clearly that a terminal with graphic capability is desirable. Similarly a light-pen or Rand-tablet type of device seems necessary for interaction. At the time of writing no *major* manufacturer, as part of its regular product line, makes a terminal device that has the necessary features at a reasonable cost. Some smaller companies[2] do offer appropriate terminals that can be driven by many types of central computer, and as these become more widely available there will be further use and experimentation.

To provide true remote capability the communications link between the terminal and main computer should be by telephone. Cable connection between the computer that does the main calculation, or has access to the main data-base, is not compatible with a general system that can be operated from any location, including one remote from the computer. There are obvious low-cost compromises, such as the PDP 8 graphics computer/terminal configuration, but these are not many in number since the major manufacturers have yet to offer such low-cost remote capability.

Central Computer

The central computer has to be able to support remote terminals but it does not necessarily have to be time shared or have a real-time data-base. Such a multiple access computer can be simulated with almost any third generation computer system, and some second generation equipment. Depending on the application there are many viable short-run solutions: this experiment used a second generation computer system with many limiting features and yet the computer was quite adequate as a support device for the managers involved. Another alternative is a multiprogrammed third generation system with the partition active for only a small portion of the day.

---

[2] For example, Computer Displays Inc., Information Displays Inc., Digital Equipment Corporation.

Data-Base

Obviously, all the information necessary for the decision process has to be in machine-sensible form. This can be done in some application areas by tapping the tape-based central information system already in use. Others may have low enough volume to permit manual key punching and others may have data already on an on-line device. In any event, there are a variety of strategies that can be used to create a data-base for terminal use. In the short run for many problems the data-base does *not* need to be maintained in real-time or necessarily on-line. This can cut the costs and effort involved considerably.

In this experiment the data were hand key punched from printed computer output of other material. Owing to some particular characteristics of the computer environment involved, this proved to be the fastest and least expensive way of getting the data. This solution was low-cost and more than accurate, and timely enough for the decision involved. In other words, many management problems have relatively little data but a lot of manipulation to handle the "what if" questions. In such situations there are a number of temporary solutions that allow the application to proceed until the on-line data-base is ready for use by the MDS.

The previous chapters have dealt fairly explicitly with the experimental environment and the conditions of the research work. Some overview of the specific findings has been provided, particularly for those findings that were regarded as most significant. There are a number of components in an MDS and eventually all have to be functioning smoothly if this tool is to become an everyday part of management's available resources. However, this does not imply that management can afford to sit back and wait until its basic MIS work is completed. There are a great many things that can be started in the meantime; for instance, projects involving an MDS that are economically viable now. Technology has changed rapidly, perhaps more rapidly than most managers realize. This experiment suggests that it is time for many companies to reevaluate the plans and progress of their MIS activity, as very often the MDS approach might well be worth the allocation of resources.

Chapter 10

MDS—The Future

THE FUTURE POSSIBILITIES OF THE MDS APPROACH look most attractive. From this experiment it seems obvious that there are at least two fruitful lines of exploration and development. The first builds on access, through the MDS, to the decision process itself.

Access to the decision process allows research on the problem-solving process and, in understanding it better, the possibility of improving the process. In addition, by having access to it, and being able to record, replay, and study the process in detail, it is possible to develop an understanding of the implicit decision rules, criteria, and models that are involved. This accessibility provides a way for continued learning and improvement over time.

The second takes advantage of the power provided by the MDS to improve the major stages of the decision process, those of intelligence, design, and choice. Each of these major stages of any problem-solving process has different requirements for computation, information, and formal models. This experiment was not very ambitious on any of these three dimensions yet enough insight has been gained to see the tremendous potential of coupling the human problem solver with some of these components.

The MDS works for this particular problem with these managers. There is no evidence to suggest that either the problem or the managers are in the least unusual. The MDS can reasonably be expected to duplicate its performance on any problem with similar characteristics. The reasons for whatever success the MDS has achieved are due in part to the fact that it relieves most of the bottlenecks suggested in Chapter 8. In more general terms it seems that the MDS helps the decision makers in the intelligence, design, and choice phases of their process in the following important ways:

INTELLIGENCE

Miller (46) maintains that interesting complex problems involve the simultaneous handling by the decision makers of at least (a) goals, (b) possible solutions and their implications, and (c) present conditions. From this experiment and the subsequent use the managers have made of the system it is clear that the MDS has taken over portions of (b) and (c), leaving the goal setting and solution creation to the managers. The portion taken over by the system has reduced the managers' load and left them time for more creative activity.

However, we can go much further than the system has done in both (b) possible solutions—discussed below, and (c) the evaluation of present conditions. It is possible to collect criteria with the process described later in this chapter, and then build these into the system so that they act as filters and provide some active help to the managers.

Similarly, the graphical features of the system were useful in detecting patterns in the data, but much more can be done in developing creative displays that portray the data to facilitate interpretation.

DESIGN

Cognitive processes generally require constant stimulus, therefore delay adversely affects decision making by sharply reducing the availability of relevant stimuli. Management decision making deals with ambiguous and incomplete data and one reason that successful decisions are made is due to the insightful characteristics of human decision makers. Therefore, if the data are coupled to insight, and manipulative power is available to test the implications of the insight, then there is a real possibility for creative problem solving. Using the MDS with its models and data-base in an interactive mode stimulates the managers to develop several solutions, to develop new alternatives. The interaction keeps the managers immersed in a rich environment of associations which can lead to efficient and productive problem solving.

This immediate response to questions or alternatives specified by the manager was a useful and significant feature of the system. There is a long way to go in software and interface design if this process is to be made as simple and powerful as is possible. The goal, of course, is to provide the ability to test alternatives without materially slowing down the manager's natural decision process, to let him see the implications of a design without causing him to slow down his thought processes.

CHOICE

The limited rationality of human decision makers that Simon[1] and others discuss can be eased if the decision maker is given additional memory and manipulative capacity. Some form of short-term memory aid seems to be useful. The MDS provides this though the control functions which allow the user to call and test various options. Similarly, as has been discussed above, his pattern recognition ability is aided by putting the information in graphical form. These simple additions to the manager's problem-solving tools allow him to handle more complex problems in shorter time and with greater flexibility than before.

In addition, the MDS relieves the decision makers of many of the problems associated with working out the implications of a particular strategy, in addition to greatly easing the interface problem between the managers, the computational power, relevant models, and the data-base. The managers are able to examine present conditions through the MDS in any way that seems appropriate to them and, after devising solutions, they can test the impact of them in a simple and immediate fashion. Providing flexible access to models and a data-base helps to augment the capabilities of the decision maker, providing him with whatever support the best of the management science techniques has to offer.

---

[1] See Simon (42).

Because of computer limitations, this experiment did not go nearly so far as was possible with bringing models into the system. Much more work is required here to begin to see the real benefits from providing the managers with powerful models. Not only can use be made of the simulation and integer programming models which have proven themselves in other settings, but the MDS offers a unique opportunity to employ Bayesian decision theory as a practical tool for operating managers. This approach to problems assumes that a decision maker's preference curve, or attitude toward risk, is available. In the past this has usually proved a damaging assumption, but with a tool such as the MDS these curves can be fairly simply developed and maintained on an operational basis. This is but one example of the opportunities that open up when such a system is available.

These three general points (intelligence, design, and choice) discussed above have their precise counterparts in the experimental results discussed in Chapter 8. They are raised again here because they appear to be of fundamental importance to the role that interactive management decision systems can play in the management decision-making process. In fact, the experiment strongly suggests that whatever success has been achieved has been because of these three points. Since these suggested impacts lie at the heart of the problem-solving process for any complex unstructured type of managerial problem, I am willing to assert that systems such as the MDS will become widespread as decision support tools.

INTELLIGENT SYSTEMS—ACCESS TO THE DECISION-MAKING PROCESS

In all of the above work, this research has been concerned with developing and testing a system to help the manager's problem-solving process. The final product, though, has one major limitation—it only responds to the user. The user can request data, or manipulation of a simple model, and can make changes to these and ask for the impact over time. However, in almost every case the user has to initiate the request, the system merely responds. What would be much more desirable would be to have the system make *suggestions* to the user. Such an active, "intelligent" participant in the decision process offers the possibility of a major contribution to the manager.

What makes this development feasible is the access to the decision process that occurs because of the capability the MDS has of monitoring itself. The decision makers execute all of their requests for information and models, as well as implement all of their solutions, through the terminal. The computer system has to execute each request and it can easily be programmed to monitor all such requests. This trace can be saved on a tape or drum for later replay.

Thus the MDS can record an entire decision sequence, which can then be analyzed slowly by those involved. The managers can examine the way they solved important aspects of the decision, or systems analysts can help check for possible decision rules. No matter how it is used the precise sequence of events that took place in solving the problem is recorded. Obviously a series of these over time or across different decisions would have a great deal of use for those interested in the fundamental steps involved in decision making. This kind of access to the decision process has not been available before.

What this does, of course, is to provide a process by which progress can be made over time. Using this kind of analysis, some extra insight can be gained concerning the key decisions that an organization has to make. Each step can be added to what is already known, and one can build a base of knowledge which remains available despite any movement of people in and out of jobs. It does not mean that each decision maker can or should use what his predecessors left. He can, however, use it as a base, and making his reasons explicit to justify a change will in turn provide more insight for him and the organization. This systematic exploration of the decision and its variables is hard for any one manager to do; pressure from daily operations does not encourage introspection. It is even less possible for the organization itself to benefit from the accumulated wisdom of its managers since so much of their knowledge is never made explicit and hence cannot be "learned" by the organization. To break out of this pattern in the direction of greater learning is clearly desirable—the MDS offers just such a possibility.

The field of "Artificial Intelligence" has been concerned for some years with developing programs that display some attributes of human intelligence.[2] There has been a great deal of work in the area, of general problem-solving programs to solve logic theorems, chess playing programs and the like. Two accomplishments in the field provide illustrations of the point being made here in relation to the MDS. One of these is the experience that Samuel[3] had in building his checkers program. This program was a set of decision rules that Samuel put in model form to play checkers against a human (or machine) opponent. The distinctive feature of his work was that he built in an evaluative function that allowed the program to "learn." That is, within limits it could classify its mistakes and remember its successful moves so that over time it built up more successful strategies and improved its own game. It moved from being a weak player to one of championship class. Being able to modify its own criterion function (again, within well-prescribed limits) turned an ordinary program into an adaptive "learning" one, one that could change itself over time. In the context of the MDS, the challenge lies in the development of this criterion function and the provision of such a flexible set of decision rules. The MDS will let us develop these in a live business setting and apply them with greater ease than under any other system. Playing checkers is totally different from business in complexity and in most dimensions. This example is only illustrative of the kind of decision rules needed to be developed if the manager is really to be helped, and it also shows the direction in which progress can be made with the help of systems such as the MDS.

A second illustration is given by Clarkson's[4] work in simulating the decision of the trust investment officer. Clarkson wanted to build a model that would simulate the investment decisions of the trust officer. By listening to the trust officer talk out loud as he made his decisions, plus extensive questioning over the tape-recorded protocols, Clarkson was able to isolate what he felt were the major decision rules. In running his computer model with his-

---

[2] For a cross section of such work see Feigenbaum and Feldman (31).

[3] See Samuel in (31).

[4] See Clarkson (13).

torical data, he showed that in fact the model did select much the same stocks as the trust officer had. Again the model had many limitations, and, of course, the stock market is much simpler than the normal business world. However, Clarkson did establish quite clearly that it is possible to take a decision which is thought to be largely judgmental and intuitive and dig out the implicit decision rules and formalize them in model form. The decision Clarkson was looking at was a great deal more complex than his simple model, but the process he went through could be done using the MDS. With such an approach and with continual monitoring and work with the decision rules as they became visible, it would be possible to build a base of decision rules which could be used to filter the raw data and provide the manager with a starting point. The managers would continue to use their intuition and judgment, but they could start from a clearer notion of the problem and with a better base of facts than they originally had.

In the future the MDS approach will provide powerful support to line managers. The support will have a significant impact on the way managers make decisions, and it offers a real breakthrough in the active support of the many complex decisions that line managers must make. To develop these systems more research is needed in order to understand enough of the issues involved to build effective and efficient systems.

Such work might have three major phases. The first of these would be analysis of the traces of the decision process. This could be both the monitoring of the display-system actions as well as a tape recording of the verbal discussion involved in the decision sessions. Replaying these tapes would allow both the managers and systems analysts to watch the re-creation of the process and in so doing, look for patterns. These patterns would be both in problem types and problem solutions. With enough work on classifying and analyzing problems it should eventually become possible to develop heuristics by which the system could recognize the problems. Thus heuristics would be developed and programmed into the system, to recognize patterns in the variables involved, and to bring them to the attention of the managers. These might be patterns that help identify a multidimensional problem, or patterns that complete a complex filtering of the data, before the decision maker starts work. The system could then present him with potential problems.

For example, it could be that in the last few years the mid-year sales behavior of the middle priced models was a good indication of the likely behavior of the whole line for the balance of the model year. Once this pattern had been recognized by analysis of past data, using the system's graphical features together with appropriate analytic models, a test could be programmed-in that would automatically be used in that period of the year. If the results of the test violated the sales figures planned for the balance of the year then the system would put the issue on its output list and display the problem to the managers.

This is perhaps an overly elaborate example; a simpler one might be to monitor sales projections, apply some relevant confidence level, and indicate to the managers when profits fell below budgeted levels. The point of these illustrations is simply to suggest that we could relieve the human decision maker of part of the problem-finding process and leave it to the system, thus freeing the manager to deal with the more significant, complex problems.

A second stage might then be not only to have the system identify patterns, but also solutions for each pattern or problem type associated with the system. These might be solutions that the managers have used on past occasions. The system, the next time such a problem pattern is recognized, could search for possible solutions, and using some heuristics developed by the managers, select the most appropriate. The system at this stage would then be identifying problems and likely solutions and presenting both to the manager. He would then select his strategy, and presumably provide feedback to the systems designer on the adequacy of the heuristics. In this way the system could evolve over time and better heuristics could be developed.

The third stage in this process would be to have the system identify problems and solutions but then evaluate the differences between the manager's final solution and the one the system originally selected. Such evaluation could eventually lead to the system modifying its own heuristics. When the system recognized a problem it would suggest a solution or range of solutions. If the manager chose to ignore the suggestion, which would probably have come from some previous decision of his, then he could go ahead and develop a new one. In either case the system would store the relevant variables and, at the end of the time period involved, it could present the actual impact together with the expected impact if another alternative had been taken. This post-decision analysis provides the manager with greater insight, and if the decision has criteria by which it can be measured then that data would provide input to an adaptive "learning" process by which the model adjusted its own heuristics.

Such an adaptive, learning type of system in support of managerial decision making would be of tremendous assistance to the decision process. The system would recognize the patterns of problem-solving behavior by its users, and when it came across a problem that had occurred before, it could interrupt the user to suggest to him an appropriate solution based on its past experience. Such adaptive learning, split between the system and the user, offers some interesting potential in moving problems toward the structured area of decision making and leaving the manager with the more challenging task of improving the quality of the decision-making process itself.

At this point the MDS would have become an active "intelligent" participant in the decision process; making suggestions, pointing out strategies, and generally being a useful and active support tool for the manager. It should be stressed that this is not going to be an easy or a rapid process. In fact stage three above may not be feasible in any real sense for a long time. However, any progress in stages one and two above would be an improvement over most current complex decision-making processes.

This experiment has shown that the tools are available and that systems can be built that will support complex unstructured decision making. Properly designed for appropriate problems, these systems can have a significant impact on the decision process. This is of importance because most of management's decisions, the unstructured decisions, have not been well supported by analysis and information in the past. There is still a great deal to be learned, but no major company can afford not to have some active program in this area. The technology is available and becoming less expensive, the major concepts and issues are clear; what is lacking is management's understanding of these concepts and their willingness to become involved. Such involvement is absolutely necessary to provide the perspective and analysis required for an effective MDS. The MDS area cannot be left to computer people or other staff personnel. It must involve line managers as active members of the team. When this occurs the payoff can be substantial. Progress in the effective use of computers in organizations in the next decade will involve this unstructured area of management decisions, and we can expect substantial impact, but each individual company will have to replan its own information system activities if it is to participate in these dramatic changes.

APPENDIX
BIBLIOGRAPHY

Appendix A

INTRODUCTION

THE MATERIAL IN THESE APPENDIXES is designed to provide more detail on certain aspects of the system. Appendixes A, B, and C should be of special interest to systems analysts or interested managers. Appendix A covers the field of display systems more thoroughly than was possible in the text. The range of systems, the way these systems work, and the kind of features that make them useful in a management setting are all discussed. All of this with a view toward facilitating the selection of a relevant terminal for management use. Appendix B covers the software goals that might be established for such a system, and Appendix C the software architecture of the MDS. The degree of modularity and ease of use of the system is heavily influenced by the way the software is constructed; for this reason there is considerable detail provided on this topic.

Appendix D contains some protocol and observation from a typical session of the actual decision situation. All discussion by the managers, as they used the system in each session, was taped and transcribed for analysis. Some of the more interesting portions of one of these sessions are also reproduced in Appendix D.

Terminal Hardware

The hardware selection process for visual-display terminals is not simple. There are many trade-offs to be made on hardware features and, of course, these are also affected by the software available. This appendix discusses the components of a visual-display terminal, one approach to the selection process in the general case, and then summarizes the characteristics of the terminal actually used in the experiment.

All visual-display devices in use as terminals have the same basic components in one form or another (Exhibit A–1). The cost difference and flexibility of the display system tends to depend on whether the component parts are all at the terminal end or whether some of the components are part of the central computer. The comparison table (Exhibit A–2) provides some further information on this. The basic display components (numbers corresponding to Exhibit A–1) are:

    (1) Display mechanism
    (2) Interaction media
    (3) Connection equipment
    (4) Core
    (5) Logic

Exhibit A–1

Basic Components of Visual Displays

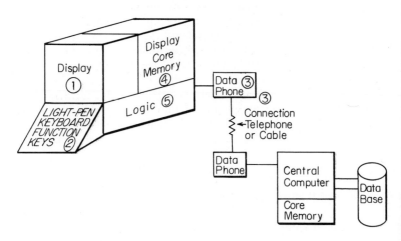

1. *Display Mechanism*

This is the mechanism by which the signals from the computer are translated to a visual display.

There are several possible display techniques that can be used; these include cathode-ray tubes, large screen projection techniques, and television systems. Of these the cathode-ray tubes have shown the greatest promise for interactive terminals thus far. The computer-driven "cathode-ray display tube has three basic components, the electron gun, the deflection system and a phosphor screen. . . ." The electron gun is comprised of a heater, cathode, grid accelerator electrode, and a focusing system. It is used to form and focus the electron beam.[1] The deflection system, employing either electrostatic plates or an electromagnetic coil, positions the beam upon the screen. The phosphor screen produces light of the desired intensity, persistence, and color.

To this basic tube are added a character-generating device and a vector-drawing capability.

There are several character-generating devices, one of the most common being that in which the character is formed, or traced, as in normal writing. This character-writing or "painting" technique makes it easier and less expensive to have different sized and shaped characters. Another alternative is the "shaped beam" or extrusion technique in which the electron beam is passed through a mask. This latter method does form a clearer character but lacks the flexibility of the pure character-generation method.

A variation on the regular CRT is the so-called "Storage Tube." These devices are more recent and have considerable promise due to their very much lower costs. The image in these devices is "stored" on a metal grid in contact with the phosphor and this maintains the image. It removes the necessity of refreshing the image and hence the need for core memory. Since core is expensive the cost can be cut very substantially. One small Cambridge firm is manufacturing and selling, at $8,000 purchase price, a storage-tube terminal that handles many of the functions of regular CRT devices selling for $75,000—a substantial reduction.

2. Interaction Media

The display console has associated with it means by which the user can interact with the system. The principal media currently available are four: keyboard, light-pen, function-keys and Rand-tablet.

The keyboard is essentially the same as a typewriter keyboard with the addition of a few keys. The keyboard may or may not have paper and printing associated with it, and is used for entering data or instructions to be sent to core memory.

The light-pen is a pencil-like object which, when activated, identifies the position on the screen at which it is pointing. This information is used in a variety of ways depending on the application and the

---

[1] Details on the CRT from Poole (55), page 4.

specifics of the hardware. Typically, when the pen is activated (by pushing a button) an interrupt is sent to the central computer which identifies that the incoming message is from the light-pen and the precise location of the interrupt. This location is identified in a table (for example), and if an entry is present the computer executes the code pointed to in the table. Thus the computer reacts, as it has been programmed, to light-pen interrupts.

Function-keys can be thought of as permanent pre-written, or wired, subroutines for specific tasks. Thus there might be a function-key to cause the screen to be blanked out, or to send the contents of a "scratch-pad" memory to the central computer, and so forth. Physically these function-keys are normally buttons, but they can be under light-pen control.

The Rand-tablet operates in a similar fashion to the light-pen. It is a pencil-like device that is used on a horizontal writing tablet placed in front of the screen. There are two modes of operation, in one the movement of the pencil causes a dot, or cursor, to move across the screen, following the path of the pencil. When the cursor is on the location the user wants, then he pushes down on the point and this sends the signal to the computer. The second mode of operation allows the user to write on the screen exactly as one would on paper. In either case the device is being used for direct graphic input and is similar to the light-pen in purpose.

3. Connection Equipment

The visual-display will normally be remote from the computer facility. Connection is by cable or via data-phones and regular voice grade telephone lines. Maximum cable lengths are normally in the order of 2,000 feet which makes them inappropriate for remote location. Telephone connection can be from any distance which means that any central computer anywhere in the world is potentially available. Since there are no mechanical operations in the display, it can handle information as fast as the line can carry it, normally 2,400 or 4,800 bits per second. Grouping lines together or using micro-wave systems are other alternatives with greater speed, but their cost is higher.

4. Core

The display device may have some form of high-speed storage (drum or core storage) at the device itself. This sharply reduces the demands on the central computer as the display is refreshed from its own core. Communication with the central system is then only necessary when the picture is to be changed. This form of stand alone display system also permits other functions to be done locally without taking central computer time. For example, a message could be typed in on the keyboard into the local core and would be displayed at some fixed part of the screen. The message can be completed, examined, edited and *then* sent to the central computer.

As was suggested above, the trade-off in selecting the type of device is heavily application dependent. The considerably higher price paid for the "stand-alone" display must be matched against the increased claims against the central computer time of the simpler display.

5. *Logic*

Certain display systems have some limited logic capability which allows certain types of decision to be made locally without recourse to the central computer. This might include interpretation of function-keys and subsequent implementation, or in the case of stand-alone displays, there might be some branch logic enabling a picture to be constructed from instructions in various different locations of display memory.

The sequence of events when a terminal having these five components is in operation is roughly as follows:

(1) A series of instructions is built by the central computer to form a display (e.g., there will be an instruction such as "display the characters, listed next, in location x, y on the screen face").

(2) In Exhibit A–2, Figure 1, this set of instructions resides in the buffer of the main core. In Figure 2 the instructions reside in the display's "stand-alone" core; and in Figure 3 either as in 2 or in the small computer core.

(3) The display unit recognizes each instruction through hardware devices and performs the required act. At the end of the set of instructions the entire picture is displayed on the face of the screen.

(4) On cathode-ray tube screens (the most common variety) the picture fades as the phosphor loses its luminescence. To avoid this, the instructions are sent again and the picture refreshed. This refreshing must occur 30 times every second if the picture is to appear flicker-free. In Figure 1 the central computer takes care of this refreshing, hence the connecting lines are constantly in use. In Figure 2 the display system refreshes itself from its own core; thus, the refreshing process does not take central computer time or use the communications lines. In

Figure 3 the refreshing comes either from display core or the small computer core.

(5) The user can interrupt the system using one of the three devices suggested. In Figure 1 this interrupt is searched for by the computer, evaluated, and an appropriate reaction made. In Figure 2 the interrupt is interpreted by the display logic and a message sent to the central computer which either (a) interrupts the computer and tells it what kind of message is involved, or (b) waits until polled by the central computer and then sends the interpreted message.

The five components discussed above are the basic elements of an interactive terminal. The exact configuration, the selection of specific characteristics for each of the five elements, is application dependent. Some of the major alternatives are discussed below.

Systems Configuration

The most basic choice in the systems configuration decision has to do with which of the two variations in the current technology are most appropriate for the application, the traditional cathode-ray tube or the storage-tube devices. The storage-tube displays[2] have three disadvantages: (1) They have smaller screens and therefore contain less information. (2) They use a Rand-tablet[3] type of graphic input as opposed to the light-pen on the CRT displays. However, a Rand-tablet is more than adequate for many applications and is simple to use. (3) They require the erasing of the whole display and redrawing it if only a part is to be erased. Offsetting these disadvantages is the much lower cost (at the moment a factor of 10:1) and the stability and clarity of the screen.

If the storage-tube variety is not adequate for the decision problem, then the other major alternative is to use the regular CRT display. This in turn involves at least three specific decisions. Exhibit A–2, Figures 1, 2, and 3 indicate the issues involved in diagrammatic form. The first issue, Figures 1 and 2, involves a decision between local and central core. Since the display has to be refreshed constantly in order to maintain a flicker-free image, this places heavy time demands on the central computer. However, if core is available locally, it increases the hardware costs of the terminal.

---

[2] For example, Computer Displays Inc. Model 1007A.

[3] See Poole (55) for details.

Exhibit A–2

Visual Displays—System Configuration

FIGURE 1

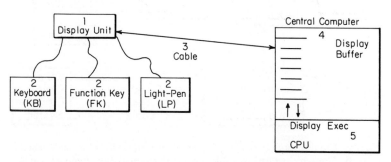

NOTES: The cable (also Figure 3) provides a wide path and hence instantaneous data transfer. This allows light-pen tracking and other high data rate applications. Maximum length of the cables is approximately 2,000 feet.

Refreshing the display 30 times a second to prevent flicker causes a heavy drain on central computer time.

FIGURE 2

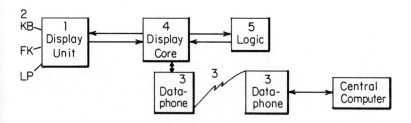

NOTES: The display device has its own core and hence refreshes itself without accessing the main computer. The cost is higher for the display than in Figure 1, but computer time is saved.

At additional cost more logic can be put in the display allowing fewer demands on the main CPU.

Telephone connection is possible, allowing any distance between terminal and computer. However, the data rate is limited and thus will not permit certain functions.

FIGURE 3

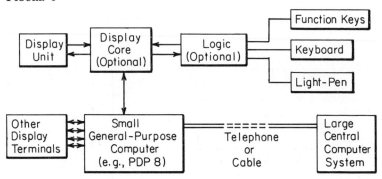

NOTES: The display device releases some of its complexity to a small general-purpose computer which is cable-connected. When the terminal cannot handle a task, it gives it to the small computer.

When the satellite computer cannot handle the task efficiently, it passes it on to the large computer. The problems of what should happen at which point in the system, and how complex each stage should be are issues that are dependent on the situation.

Similarly, the contrast between configurations in Figures 2 and 3 raises the issue of how much logical capability should be available locally, and, by implication, whether the central computer should be relieved from some of the more trivial computation. This logical capability includes the use of scratch-pad entries as well as computational logic on the application itself.

The third major choice is telephone versus cable connection between the terminal and the computer that derives it. Cable has a maximum length of 2,000 feet, so true remote applications are only possible via telephone. In Figure 3 an example is given of one of many points on the spectrum of logic/core trade-offs. In this instance, the cable connects up to seven terminals to one block of core and logic (for example a PDP 8i computer) and this small remote computer has access via telephone lines to large-scale computational power and large data files in the main computer system.

Clearly, all of these three trade-offs in Exhibit A–2 are applications dependent. The particular demands of the application will determine which configuration is the most attractive. Access to a large central data-base or heavy computational requirements have different hardware requirements than, say, the need for local data and simple search procedures.

Appendix A

Evaluation of these requirements will narrow the range of possible terminals down to a very few. For example, as of the time of writing, IBM and GE companies do not offer graphical terminals that can be telephone-connected directly to a remote computer. Several small firms do, but they may have other undesirable characteristics.

With the range narrowed, it is then possible to look at specific attributes which affect the information content and communication ability of the terminal. One strategy for evaluating this consistently is to take Exhibit A–3 and for each display that meets the macro specifications discussed above, assess the degree to which each terminal meets the job requirements along the dimensions listed on the left. That is, assess how important each dimension is to the application at hand, and then assess how well the terminal provides that capability. This approach forces consideration of all characteristics and provides the opportunity for in-depth analysis.

The Visual-Display Device Used

The visual-display device used in this project was an IDI (Information Displays Incorporated) terminal and was located in the headquarters building of the company concerned. It was connected via a data-phone set and telephone lines to the central computer facilities which house the Univac 494s and other equipment of the central system. The 494 computer has associated with it large data files which are used by the company's real-time system for the collection of sales and financial data.

The display device consists of the three main components in Exhibit A–4. The physical arrangement is two units, one the screen and the other the core and logic units. These various components are discussed below:

Cathode-Ray Tube (CRT)

This is a 21-inch cathode-ray tube with a light-pen attachment. The tube produces a flicker-free picture with enough intensity to be clearly visible in a room with normal lighting.

The display generator hardware puts out signals which cause the desired display to be "painted" on the CRT face. Thus the letter "A" for example is traced out or drawn on the phosphor screen of the CRT. This is in contrast to systems where the letters or characters are formed with dots or extruded characters. This painting process provides a great deal of flexibility as the hardware can be adapted to produce any conceivable special character.

Comparison Chart—Visual Display Terminals

	Computer Displays ARDS	IMLAC PDS-1	IBM 2260	IDI 1009	IBM 2250-1	Adage Agt-30
Purchase Price[1] High	8,000	20,245	20,325	80,000	95,960	175,000
Low	7,000	8,900	17,715		72,165	125,000
Screen Size (Inches)[2]	8.25 × 6.4	11.5 × 8	9 × 4	13 × 13	12 × 12	14 × 14
Storage Capacity (Characters)[3]	4,000	4–64K	960	5,120	3,848	16,000
Addressable Points[4]	1081 × 1415	1024 × 1024	Not App.	1024 × 1024	1024 × 1024	128K × 128K
Character Rate	500	41,600		75,000	67,000	78,000
Gen. Technique[5]	7 × 9 Dot	5 × 7 or 7 × 9 Dot	5 × 7 Dot	Stroke	Stroke	Stroke
Max. Data Rate (Char./Sec.)[6]	500	500,000	2,560	Variable	475,000	500,000
Character Rotation[7]	No	No	No	Yes	No	No
Hard Copy[8]	Opt.	Opt.	No	Yes	No	Opt.
Graphic Input[9]	Opt.	Opt.	No	Yes	No	Yes
Vector Capability	Yes	Yes	No	Yes	Yes	Yes

Function Keys[10]	No	No	No	Opt.	Opt.	Yes
Keyboard[11]	58 Key ASC 11	Typewriter	50-Key Typewriter	Opt.	Opt. Typewriter	Teletype
Max. Characters Per Line[12]	80 or 50	72 or 64	80 or 12	130 or 64	74 or 52	112 or 72
Max. Characters Flicker Free[13]	4,000	1,300	960	3,333	2,200	2,600

[1] Purchase Price is the manufacturer's list price in quantities of one for a usable range of options.

[2] Screen Size is the published viewable screen dimensions.

[3] Storage Capacity is the maximum number of characters which may be stored in the terminal for display.

[4] Addressable Points describe the number of discrete points which may be used in the horizontal and vertical directions.

[5] Character Rate and Generation Technique are the maximum rates at which characters are written on the screen and the method used to generate these characters.

[6] Maximum Data Rate is the maximum rate at which characters may be stored at the terminal.

[7] Character Rotation is the option which allows characters to be written both vertically and horizontally on the screen.

[8] Hard Copy provides a method for connecting a page printer to the terminal for printing textual material.

[9] Graphic Input is normally provided with a light-pen, mouse, rand tablet, or similar device. This option provides the user with the ability to point to, or draw, objects on the screen.

[10] Function Keys provide a separate keyboard or set of switches to indicate special functions to the computer.

[11] Keyboard is the textual input facility.

[12] Maximum Characters Per Line describe the largest number of characters in the horizontal direction.

[13] Maximum Characters Flicker Free constitute the number of characters which may be displayed before the user can observe flicker from the screen refreshing cycle.

Exhibit A–4

Project Terminal—Logical Description

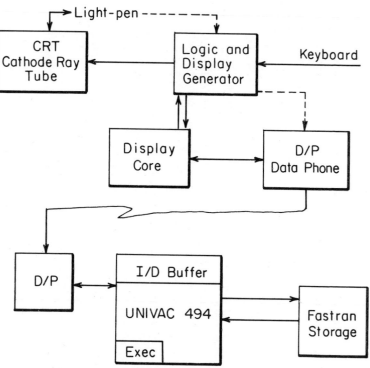

Attached to the CRT is a light-pen; this is a light-sensitive photo-cell device with an "enable" button on the pen itself. When depressed the "enable" button permits the transmission of the location of the displayed word at which it is pointing. Response on the screen is by the blinking of the character at which the pen is pointing as long as the enable button is depressed. The light-pen signal is sent from the logic/display generator unit to the central system. It contains identification as to type (light-pen) and location (IDI memory location of the word that contained the instruction to display the element at which the pen was pointing).

Display Generator

The display generator contains the logic unit and the hardware necessary to create the signals for the CRT that will result in specific functions being performed. The display generator includes the following significant features which were considered to be the minimum set necessary if the device was to be used in a management setting:

1. Character Generator—ability to generate all numerical and alphabetical characters plus a set of special characters. This is an open-ended set.
2. Vector Generator—one vector instruction draws a line from the position the beam was last in to the position specified in the instruction. There is, therefore, also a "position" command which moves the beam to the location specified without writing.
3. Size Control—there are four available sizes for the alpha-numeric characters. The smallest size allows:
   Number of characters across screen   132
   Number of characters down screen   70
4. Intensity Control—anything displayed on the tube face can be of either high or low intensity. The low intensity is bright enough to be seen in normal room lighting.
5. Line Structure—vectors or circles can have any one of the four line structures—solid, dotted, dashed, dot-dash.
6. Blink—any item on the tube face can be blinked continuously.

Core Memory

The display operates under control of its reiterative core memory. The words in core are read out starting from the beginning, and proceeding consecutively to the end where there is a jump to the beginning. This natural sequence can be altered when a "jump-to" instruction is encountered. At that point the address in the jump instruction is read out and the sequence proceeds from there. Thus, with an appropriate series of jumps, it is possible to build a picture from a series of fragmented instruction sets in the display core memory in several ways:

1. From the computer via the data-phone. Data can be sent to any location or series of locations by the transmission of the address of the first word and then all succeeding words for that segment following sequentially.
2. Data can also be entered or changed by using the light-pen to interrogate a displayed character. The word and its address appear on lighted push-button indicators which can then be changed appropriately.
3. Scratch-pad entry is also possible. The last 27 of the 4,096 words in memory are used as a scratch-pad memory, providing for the

storage of two lines of 64 characters each of alpha-numeric data. A portion of the display core is reserved and anything typed in on the keyboard enters that portion of core, is displayed automatically on the last two lines of the screen, and can subsequently be sent to the computer as a message. A function-key (push button) transmits the contents of the scratch pad to the central computer via the data-phone.

Data-Phone

This is the standard Bell System device Model 201 B with a capacity of 2,400 bits per second. The terminal is limited in this case by the transmission capability of the data-set. There are a variety of methods of overcoming this, such as the new data-sets and the Telpak and other wide-band transmission techniques, but all of these are more expensive and the available speeds were adequate for this application.

Central Computer

The central computer facility is a pair of Univac 494 systems. These have evolved from an original 490 computer used for switching teletype messages in 1962. The present system is a multiple access interrupt system where the remote device interrupts the processor whenever it is ready to send. The processor checks the priority of the message and inserts it in the relevant queue. Once processing begins, the message is worked on until completion with the exception of the interrupts noted above. The MDS had the highest priority available, so response time was never greater than a second or two and more normally appeared instantaneously. Processing and transmission time, of course, were in addition to response time and with the present system did not run over nine seconds for a large complex display. From the standpoint of the MDS, the Univac 494 has the following features:

1. Total response time varying with load but seldom greater than ten seconds for a complete display due to the high priority assigned to interrupts from the device.
2. A reserved segment of core, which cannot be read or written by other programs, of 10,000 words.
3. A reserved area of fastran, drum storage, for data files of ten million positions.

The Univac 494 treated the MDS as it did all of its other interrupts and therefore required no further modification to its software.

Conclusions

Our experience with the terminal was satisfactory over the three years of operation. The rate of technological change is bringing the costs down sharply for new terminals, and it is clear that hardware will not be a serious limitation for any potential user. The features with which the terminal, used in the experiment, was equipped seemed a necessary and largely sufficient set. There were numerous minor problems and some reliability issues, but the terminal was adequate for the experimental task.

It is important to note that many graphical terminals were designed as engineering tools and as such have little direct relevance for helping to solve management problems. The terminal characteristics described here are a minimum set for management use and, although they are *not* usually available as standard equipment from the large manufacturers, other manufacturers do provide them and they can be connected to any central computer that accepts terminals.

Appendix B

SOFTWARE GOALS

The Management Decision System (MDS) was designed to be used by line (or staff) managers with no computer experience. The types of problems for which it was intended have been discussed in detail in the text, but basically the MDS was meant as an aid for one of the most difficult types of problems managers face: that is, for those management problems that are large, unstructured, nonprogrammable (in Simon's terms) and that involve management judgment.

In order to be effective in such an environment it was felt that the software for the system had to have the following characteristics:

1. Simple to Operate

The system had to be simple enough to use so that an executive with no computer knowledge and a busy schedule could use it comfortably. This requires the hardware characteristics noted in Appendix A as well as important software considerations. The basic trade-offs in software are to provide a system with fast reaction time that is powerful enough to be of real benefit to the user, yet requires a minimum amount of the user's time to specify the problem and interpret the answer.

2. General Purpose

The system developed had to be applicable to any part of a business. Since the terminals might be used in any aspect of an organization, the software should be completely application independent. This increases the uses to which the terminals can be put in any one organization.

3. *Modular*

The system has to be able to absorb changes in software to allow for the addition of different types of displays or the use of different forms of data. The insertion or deletion of any one package should not affect the others in any way whatsoever, thus an application programmer can install an application in one location without regard to any other location.

4. *Open Ended*

There should be no limitation on the number of types of functions that can be added to the system. As specific capabilities (e.g., exponential smoothing; rescaling graph; factor analysis; etc.) are required, they must be added without losing other functions or requiring changes to the basic structure.

5. *Hardware Independent*

The concept and structure of the Management Decision System should not be dependent on one particular computer or hardware configuration. Clearly the specific implementation will be dependent on the hardware and software of a specific machine; the basic system, however, should be structured to be applicable to any multiple-access system and should also be programmed to as large an extent as possible in some machine-independent language.

6. *Interactive*

The system should respond readily to user requests. This involves a sophisticated guidance and editing section to prompt the user as to necessary actions and to screen out the more obvious human errors. The nature of the interaction must not act as a hindrance in the problem-solving process. The range of action open to the user must be broad enough to encompass all useful action he can take in the course of his problem-solving process. The specification of such actions to the system must be in a language he understands and in a form that lends itself to short unambiguous specification time and fast responses.

The design of the management-decision system had to be such as to allow the above six features to exist to as great a degree as possible. Clearly *some* of these goals have been sought and largely attained in systems such as IBM's 360 O/S, MIT's OPS and so forth. In this instance, however, the emphasis is on the user and handling his needs without the intermediary of a normal compiler language. In short the system had to handle the language of the manager and interpret it to form a suitable display. Due to this emphasis on the user, the system, above all else, had to be interactive. Experience in designing executive programs for interactive forms of computer systems is slight and what does exist is concerned with the central computer and its operation rather than executive programs covering the combination of the user, the terminal, and the central computer. Unfortunately, without a base to build on, these goals could not be realized to as great a degree as was desirable. However, a working system was built which achieved some minimum level of accomplishment in each of the six areas.

The six goals were met to some degree in the process of implementation. As can be seen from the discussion that follows, a great deal more effort has to be expended on the software-design problem before any evaluation can be made as to optimal implementation schemes. A few of the salient points in this particular implementation are discussed opposite each of the six objectives.

1. *Simple to Operate*

A characteristic of the interaction is that it must be simple yet powerful—where powerful implies many machine functions implemented for every one user action. In previous systems there has always been an attempt to strive for the many machine actions for one user's statement or request, frequently with much success. This has usually been in the context of compilers where the many-for-one translations did not take place until the user had created some unambiguous source language coding. The system in this instance has to respond to general purpose commands with specific instructions to create a particular display.

The solution to this, discussed in detail at a later point, is to design the system so that light-pen responses can be used to select relevant alternatives from among those available. From a given position there are a series of possible branches—the light-pen is used to select the path the user wishes to follow, and the system automatically keeps track of the choices he has made. This information then becomes data for the system which allows its general purpose routines to develop specific displays.

2. *General Purpose*

This objective is one sought by all systems that translate the user's desires to the computer, and is reflected by the continuing efforts to develop an all-purpose language, of which PL–1 is an example. In a similar fashion an attempt has been made to keep the structure of the Management Decision System from being special purpose. To term it a "management language" is too strong, but it has been designed to be independent of any application area. This is achieved in part by the modular and open-ended features discussed next but also by the deliberate design of a system that best meets the needs of the principal management function, that of decision making or problem solving. The structure of decision making is discussed in the text in Chapter 3 where it is asserted that at any level in the organization a simple modification of Simon's basic Intelligence, Design, and Choice phases usefully represent the process. By designing the Management Decision System to facilitate work in these areas, the hope is that a system has been created that is general purpose in the management area.

Search

The search facility is implemented by:

(a) Allowing the user to specify any data he wishes with the light-pen.
(b) Having the system organize the data with utility routines.
(c) Having the data processed with mathematical routines to present it in a variety of ways.
(d) Allowing the user to jump to any legal operation in the process (with the light-pen).
(e) Availability of wide range of data formats, including graphs, so that pattern recognition is facilitated.

Design

(a) Light-pen specification of any display format desired.
(b) System or light-pen use of a wide variety of mathematical routines to process the data.
(c) Ability to allow the user to enter or change data at will.

Choice

(a) Direct identification and selection of alternatives with the light-pen.
(b) Specification of any data with light-pen.
(c) Specification of data display format with light-pen, so that different variables can be compared.

3. Modular

This objective of the display system is achieved in a manner that has proved successful in other fields. There exists a set of driving tables which form a common interface to which all other routines are connected. This allows the addition of any other routines, either macro types or simple subroutines. Similarly, since the executive system finds all of its data in the driving tables, the executive system itself can have additions made to it. Ideally, of course, these modifications should come from the programs themselves. This self-adaptive mode is quite possible but it is not a practical or desirable first step. The particular hardware used imposed severe limitations, and the need to develop a first-order functioning system before embarking on more ambitious projects made it undesirable to attempt to implement this self-adaptive response initially.

4. Open-Ended

As implied in 3 above, this feature of the system is not unique and has worked very successfully in other systems—the MIT OPS–3 is a good example. This feature as implemented here is discussed in the following chapter and like the modular feature above, it is not in its most refined form.

5. Hardware Independent

Hardware independence in this instance implies that the basic structure and logic of the system are not dependent on the hardware being used. The original coding of this structure was in machine language due to hardware resources available. This was subsequently recoded in COBOL which provided a degree of machine independence.

The system appears to be applicable to any multiple-access terminal system with a visual-display terminal of the type indicated as appropriate in Appendix A.

6. Interactive

The Management Decision System has to have this interactive capacity. The form of interaction should be up to the user; he should have all three basic types available (light-pen, keyboard, function-keys). To keep the interaction simple and have a general-purpose system requires some care in systems design. Otherwise there is danger of programming the software for specific interrupts only.

The approach used was to have tables linking the display type, location of interrupt, and appropriate response. These tables could be built by the system, or specified by the programmer, and resulted in entries being made in the driving tables. The entries are in turn interrogated by the executive system and appropriate responses made.

In summary it can be said that, with the exception of the interaction objectives, the others (1, 2, 3, 4, 5) have been achieved elsewhere. However, it is suggested that the combination of these, with a system oriented around problem solving and having the interaction capability demonstrated here, is a unique combination.

Working with machine language in a visual-display, problem-solving environment is at least as awkward as when writing regular business programs. The added efficiency of machine language is completely inadequate compensation for the added mass of detail that has to be coded and kept track of in the old familiar way. On-line modification to a higher level language and the ability to recompile from a remote terminal are desirable features. With these, programming can become efficient enough to support management terminal activity.

IMPLEMENTATION—HARDWARE

The hardware features required for a managerial terminal were discussed at some length in Appendix A. Experience with implementation indicated that there are three hardware characteristics which are of particular importance. These three attributes of the hardware are those that were especially significant (or limiting) in this application and might be expected to be so in other problem environments.

Screen Size

Both the screen size and the character size have a significant effect on the information (and data) that can be portrayed. The screen size used, 21 inches, seemed to be the minimum acceptable size for a large complex problem. It was not close to the maximum point where the user is unable to assimilate everything on the tube face. Experiments will have to be run to determine this point, but with the type of information being displayed in this instance, it appears as though the information content of a 30-inch screen, or its equivalent, would be more satisfactory.

Character size and vector resolution are obviously related to this issue. The smallest character used in this implementation is visible to three or four people grouped around the screen. With a 21-inch screen, 140 characters could be displayed across the screen. This seemed to be a minimum acceptable level and, at least in this application, anything less would have been most undesirable. For example, if the user is looking at a one-year time span with six digit numbers, then there have to be about 120 positions on the screen if everything is to be portrayed.

2. Reliability

Hardware reliability is an obviously desirable characteristic. To the extent that on-line interaction is involved, the user can become extremely frustrated by malfunctioning hardware. This situation will improve over time but it can be aggravating, and to the extent that top management is a user, then it becomes even more important to have it working. To have a display terminal "wipe-out" half way through a meeting of managers who are depending on it for support in the decision-making process is not very satisfactory.

3. Flicker-Free Rate

The flicker-free rate has an important, and obvious, bearing on the amount of information that can be displayed. If the entire display is blinking, then any user finds it awkward to use the information contained in the display.

The amount of information that can be displayed without appearing to flicker is a function of several factors. In fact, the following dimensions have to be traded-off to arrive at an optimal solution; phosphor type, ambient lighting, character generation rate, core speed, and core size.

(a) Phosphor type: The low decay-rate phosphors (i.e., those that stay bright for longer) require higher energy levels and they cannot be focused as finely; resolution is poor.

(b) Ambient lighting: The greater the amount of light in the room, the more frequently the picture has to be regenerated to avoid the appearance of flicker. Thus, if a display is flickering and then the room lights are turned off, the flicker will be less pronounced or disappear altogether.

(c) Character generation rate: The speed with which the character generator, or the vector generator, operates is also a relevant factor. All other things being equal, the display system with the fastest generator can display more information before flicker is noticeable. Comparisons among equipment are made difficult due to the variation in reporting by equipment manufacturers. The length of time to generate a short line, long line, and character are all different, and since any given display has a different mixture of these, it is difficult to predict performance.

(d) Core Performance: The access time to display core and the amount of core to be cycled through have an obvious relationship to the performance of the display. This application had the following characteristics:

Character Generator = 14 microseconds/character
Display core access = 5 microseconds/word
Number of instructions in typical display = 600–1500 words.

Appendix C

SOFTWARE ARCHITECTURE

Management Decision System—Functional Structure

Before examining the functional structure of the entire system a word should be said about the physical arrangements. The central computer was located at the Tele-computer Center about 15 miles from the Corporate Headquarters building. The terminal itself was in the headquarters building but could have been located anywhere in the world as the connection was by regular telephone line.

Major components of this system are shown in Exhibit C–1. The logical connections in this system are discussed in the next section. I. (The Roman numerals refer to the section so marked in Exhibit C–1.)

(a) The main core memory of the central Univac 494 system has an assigned and protected segment of core for the management display system.

(b) In addition there is a privileged segment of core for the central computer's supervisory program. This supervisory program performs a large number of functions, but the ones of particular concern here are simply:

1. Senses all interrupts, checks their priority against the program in execution and makes a decision about the disposition of the interrupt.

2. Handles all I/0 requests from other programs, e.g., if information is required from the Fastran storage, the MDS program requests this from the main supervisor which in turn performs the necessary functions to retrieve the data from the Fastran.

EXHIBIT C–1

Hardware Layout with Major Logic

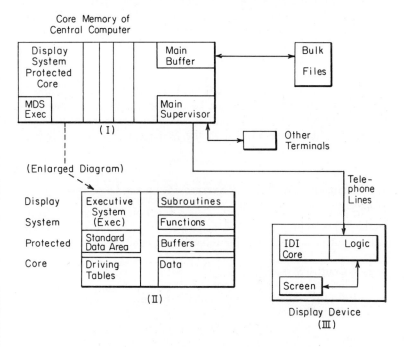

3. The main buffer area is used by the supervisor as an area in which to read or write the I/0 request of the operating programs that request Fastran operations. In addition, of course, the supervisor initiates I/0 requests of its own, principally those of swapping programs in and out of core. The user programs specify where this main buffer will be so that its physical location in core is flexible.

II. The segment of main core in the central computer that is protected for the MDS device is divided into several segments. These segments can be of varying sizes depending upon the application in question. For example, there may be more subroutines required for an application than there is space. In such a case the subroutine required, if not already in core, would be read in as an overlay. This dynamic core allocation is handled in the third generation equipment as part of the data management system that comes with the computer.

In this initial implementation on the Univac 494 system these functions had to be programmed, but as they are not likely to be of continuing interest they will not be pursued further here.

All of these various components of the Management Decision System that reside in the display system protected core are discussed later in this appendix.

III. The visual-display device itself has been described in Appendix A and requires no further discussion beyond pointing out that the path from the display device to the central computer terminates in the main supervisor which then relays it to the Management Decision System executive.

Management Decision System—General Description

The flow chart in Exhibit C–2 is a functional and logical layout of the MDS. This is discussed in greater detail in the material that follows but in summary has the following six components:

1. *Executive System*
   This skeleton program monitors the interaction and passes control to the relevant subparts of the system.
2. *Driving Tables*
   These specify the exact set of operations necessary to provide the user with the picture he wants at any moment in time. The required entries can be made by subroutines or the user.
3. *Specification Displays*
   A display on the tube-face on which the user can specify with the light-pen the exact data and type of display he wishes to see.
4. *Data*
   A complete data-base containing all information necessary for the problem. The data are maintained and used on Fastran drums.
5. *Subroutines*
   The specific sets of programs necessary to draw graphs, do arithmetic calculations, etc. There are several levels of complexity for these.
6. *Functions*
   These are programs that allow the user to interact with the information on the screen. They permit whatever interaction is necessary to solve the problem.

Exhibit C–2

Management Decision System—General Functional Layout

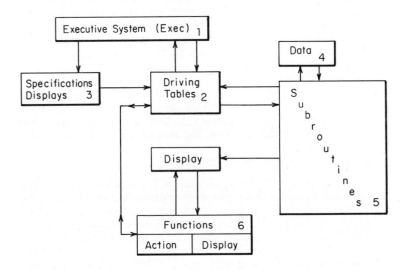

Flow-Chart Discussion

The flow-chart in Exhibit C–2 is a functional and logical arrangement of the Management Decision System. The interrelationship of the main elements is shown in the schematic, but no attempt is made to provide details. The description that follows is intended to provide an understanding of the main purpose and operation of each of the components.

Basic Structure

1. *Executive System (Exec)*

The Management Decision (MDS) runs under an operating system that provides the connection between the MDS and the central computer executive system. In this respect it provides input-output information to the main executive and receives interrupt messages from the executive and interprets them. The Exec also provides the skeleton necessary for control of the MDS. It initializes the various tables and brings in the specifications displays that are needed, as well as interpreting the tables to provide the necessary sequence in running the subroutines.

2. Driving Tables

The system is driven by tables in which all parameters are stored. These parameters are initially set by the specifications displays and some original programming. As each routine is run it interprets various parameters and then points to the next routine required by current conditions. When the new routine starts execution, its first action is to inspect the tables for the values it requires and to ascertain the status of the system in order to select an appropriate response. The tables, then, act as an interface between all segments of the system. This allows complete modularity as no routine is in any way directly dependent on any other. The other significant advantage of the table approach is that it is a very convenient structure with which to allow the user to specify his parameters at time of use.

3. Specifications Displays

In the version of the MDS used in the experiment there were two levels of specifications displays—Initialization and Specification. These are discussed in detail below but essentially they are alphanumeric tables providing the user with lists of the options open to him. With the light-pen he points to, or hits, the items he wishes and with each light-pen hit an interrupt is transmitted to the MDS containing the address of that interrupt. By a table look-up procedure an appropriate entry is made in the driving tables. When finished with the specifications displays the Exec is signaled and control passes to it.

4. Data Files

Source data would normally be in the form of mass storage most appropriate for its frequency of use. This hierarchical structure of data storage would start with high-speed drums and move down through regular disks and drums to the data-cell variety of mass storage. The data-management routines would then manipulate this information, arranged in an associative memory type of schema, to form a working data base. In this initial implementation the data base is relatively small and naturally hierarchical. Therefore, for simplicity it was only on Fastran storage and was brought in by a call from the display Exec to the main executive. It was then placed in the working data-base area. Data were brought in from this file to the I/0 buffer, manipulated by appropriate subroutines and placed in the Standard Data Area (SDA) for use by the display subroutines.

5. Subroutines

The subroutine section contains an entirely open-ended set of routines that fall into the following categories:

(a) Display subroutines.
(1) Display Subroutines—Device Independent.
This group of routines is concerned with the logic necessary to generate the data needed for the display structure per se, as opposed to the data used by the system and shown as information in the display. For example, the logic necessary to build grid lines for a graph, including the scaling and label-generating operations would fall in this device-independent category. These routines use information from the driving tables and SDA and are largely independent of the specific display being generated. For example, the grid-generating routine works for any range of values and any type of graph.
(2) Display Subroutines—Device Dependent
These routines are concerned with building the physical display words that are transmitted to the display core memory as instructions. These routines are, quite obviously, entirely dependent on the nature of the central computer system, in this case the Univac 494, and the specific visual-display device being used.

(b) Mathematical Subroutines
These routines are used to manipulate the basic data to the form required for display. They operate from the Standard Data Area (SDA) or I/0 buffer and their output is inserted in the SDA. The routines can include any mathematical function necessary for the application in question, but typically would be such routines as exponential smoothing, cumulation, averaging, factor analysis, etc.

(c) Utility Subroutines.
These routines are principally concerned with housekeeping for the system. They take care of such functions as sorting data, rearranging data files, determining largest and smallest values in files, etc. The routines are given a number and called by the Exec as necessary.

6. *Functions*

This is an open-ended set of routines that allow the user to interact with the device. Through the use of the functions, the user generates or modifies displays to help him solve his problem. The exact set of those needed for any one problem will vary with the specific problem and the user. Those functions designed for the problem under investigation are described below.

The range of such routines is limited only by the ingenuity of the programmer and the amount of core available. These routines are central to the whole terminal concept as they provide the necessary interaction between the user and the system. There are two principal types of functions: display functions, and action functions. Display functions insert user requests into the relevant portion of the driving table, they do not actually result in any visible action. To implement the changed driving table, the user requests an action function, which steps through the driving table allowing those portions that have changed to be implemented and displayed on the screen. Action functions also initiate a series of routines for certain other actions such as returning to the specifications display. These are discussed in the sections that follow.

<h2 style="text-align:center">Management Decision System—Specific Description</h2>

The discussion below is numbered according to the flow chart (Exhibit C–3). The flow chart is designed to show the overall design and the principal logical connections between the various major elements of the system. Details of this system, including a discussion of the major tables used in the system and their purpose, are available elsewhere.[1] This section is merely designed to show the software architecture used to build the MDS.

1. *Executive System*

The central computer's executive system turns over control to the MDS's executive system upon receipt of any form of interrupt. Normally this would be a light-pen (L-P) interrupt, or a typed-in instruction from the keyboard, or a turning over of control from a subprogram.

Once in control the executive system examines the status section of the driving tables and determines the type of interrupt it is responding to (by table look-up). This will be either light-pen response requesting initialization procedures to begin or else an L-P response from the functioning system.

The executive system functions by examining the various status tables and if running mode is indicated, it selects the next routine to be run from a list of routines awaiting execution and then turns control over to that routine. If running mode is not indicated, then the Exec sits in a neutral mode waiting for a further interrupt.

On the initial path, as part of the start-up procedures, the Exec displays a fixed set of displays which provide a medium for the user to specify variables to the system. These displays can be recalled later by control point option and any or all of the information changed. The information specified by these displays is entered into the driving tables.

---

[1] See Morton (50a).

Exhibit C–3

Management Decision System—Software Structure

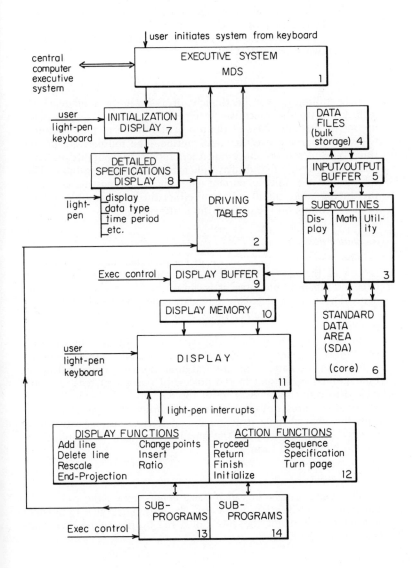

2. Driving Tables

The entries are principally made from the initialization and graph displays. All items in the table remain as is until they are replaced specifically or the system is shut down. The tables act as an interface for all the subroutines, which draw their parameters from the tables. The tables are altered by the function subprograms which make the appropriate entries in the tables, after which they pass control to the Exec which in turn examines the tables to determine what action to take.

3. Subroutines

Each subroutine can be thought of as having a number which identifies it to the executive system. The executive system picks up one of these numbers at the top of the queue in the "routines-to-be-run" slot and executes that routine. The routines are of the three types described above and their inputs and outputs are confined to the I/0 buffer, display buffer, SDA, and driving table. The subroutines are fully re-entrant and obtain all parameters from the driving table and all data from either the basic data files or the SDA depending on the class of the routine.

4. Data Files

The structure of these files is of considerable importance to the success of the MDS. There is no one solution to the problem of data file organization, since it is always highly application dependent. The existing data-base and data-collection facilities help to determine what is feasible, along with the other factors discussed in Chapter 2.

In this particular instance the data-base maintained by the corporation is very large and although quite amenable to on-line collection and manipulation, the physical limitations of central hardware time (which is old and in the process of being updated) did not make this economical. As a result the data for this application are inserted, via cards, onto the Fastran and stored there in table form. This hierarchical table structure is preferred to an associative-type schema simply because of the small size of the data and their natural hierarchical form.

5. I/0 Buffer

This buffer can be of variable size depending on the core available and the application in question. Its only function is to provide a fixed repository for the data called for by the subroutines and initiated by the Exec.

6. *Standard Data Area* (SDA)

This is a segment of core which always contains data in a form appropriate for the display subroutines. It is placed in the area as a result of the mathematical or utility subroutines. Having the data always in appropriate form, although there may be more or less than required, allows the display routines to be used on any application.

7. *Initialization Display*

This display contains alpha-numeric text of any length or arrangement desired. Opposite each item of text is a control point which when touched with the light-pen enters that item in the appropriate slot in the driving table. This can be done indefinitely, the latest choice for any slot being the one in effect at any given time. When all needed selections have been made the "proceed" control-point is hit and control passes to the executive system which checks to see that enough information has been specified for the system to proceed, generally one item per column. If there is not enough information, an appropriate error message is generated. If there is sufficient, the executive brings in the detailed specifications display.

8. *Detailed Specifications Display*

One of the options selected in 7 was the type of display desired. The executive system examines this location and brings in the appropriate detailed specifications display. If this had been selected as "graph," for example, then the display would contain alpha-numeric text appropriate for specification of parameters for a graphical display. These would be selected and inserted in the driving tables as in 7 above. The trade-off between what the user has to type in on the keyboard as specification data and what he can select directly is a function of the application. If the possible values for the parameters are few and known precisely then they can all be displayed and each item selected. If this is not the case some of the data may have to be typed in as this typing process will turn out to be more efficient than many pages of specifications displays.

9. *Display Buffer*

This is an area in core in which the subroutines, responsible for building the display instruction words, store their output. Each display is formed by a series of instructions to the unit itself. These instructions are built (30 bit words) by the display subroutines in response to the executive system and are stored sequentially in the buffer until the executive system turns control over to the main computer's supervisory system. The main supervisor transmits the correct number of words to the display's core memory. If the buffer should fill before the executive system gains control, then the running program is automatically interrupted, the buffer transmitted, and control returned to the running program.

10. *Display Memory*

This is a stand-alone core memory of 4,000 words. The unit has some limited jump logic so it is able to connect up different segments in core to form a single display. The executive system maintains a constant tally of the last IDI core location used, the location of the various display segments in the core, and so forth. This is necessary because light-pen interrupts on certain control points do no more than alter jump instructions (to miss out or add in a segment of instructions in core), and the executive system has to be aware of where these are. This ability to form a different display by merely altering a jump instruction provides extremely rapid response time as it is only necessary to transmit one or two words over the telephone lines connecting the display core to the computer.

11. and 12. *Display*

The display unit itself, as is discussed in Appendix A, has two methods by which the user can communicate with the system—the keyboard and the light-pen. The keyboard entries are transmitted, when the message is complete, by means of a manual key. The display unit cycles through its memory and maintains a "flicker-free" image on the screen.

Each light-pen interrupt results in an address being returned to the executive system. By means of a table look-up it is ascertained if the address is legal and what type of response is appropriate. Generally, responses are of two types; call for a display function, or an action function. If the request is for a display function, the executive system expects a series of light-pen interrupts which provide data to the driving tables. There is no action taken after a display function interrupt, the system simply waits for a further similar interrupt or for an action-function interrupt. After one, or a series, of display functions interrupts, the user must hit an action-function control point, normally "proceed," in order to have his display functions implemented.

The action functions cause an entry of a routine number to be made in the driving tables. This routine, which may in turn call other routines, is then implemented. For example, when the "proceed" action function is hit with the light-pen the temporary light-pen data table is inserted into the driving table and the entire plotting sequence (if graph) begun from the very beginning.

A very brief verbal description of the principal "display" and "action" function is given below.

13. *Subprograms—Display Function*

These routines are identified in the table look-up procedure following the light-pen interrupt and the correct one pointed to in the driving table. The Exec then executes the routine, and in most cases this simply sets up the reception area for the interrupt data that are to follow. Each of these routines ends by leaving the executive system in a neutral state, waiting for further information.

(a) Add or Delete Curve.

A particular curve is either added or deleted from the display. The curve is selected by light-pen and its status (on, off) reversed when hit.

(b) Rescale.

The light-pen is used to select two points on the x axis of the graph. These points are then used as the extremes of the x axis and the entire display is replotted. The original display is brought back by hitting the "return" control point which brings back the previous display.

(c) End Projection.

On a cumulative graph this routine draws a straight line between the point identified with the light-pen on any portion of a curve to any point on the right-hand "y" axis. The value on the right-hand axis is typed in on the keyboard.

(d) Change Points.

Any point on a particular curve is identified with the light-pen and a new value is typed in on the keyboard. The curve is then replotted using this new value when the "proceed" function has been hit. The "return" control point brings back the previous display.

(e) Insert.

This special-purpose function inserts sets of changed and accepted data into the basic files. These files are write-protected during all normal operations, a "carbon copy" being used for all operations of the display system. This display function is only used when the decision maker is satisfied he has a finished result and wishes to save it.

(f) Ratio.

This function alters sets of numbers by either ratios or fixed percentages. This is particularly useful if a whole file of information is to be changed by a given amount, or if the detailed breakdown of a cumulative figure is to be changed by a constant percentage to total to the newly developed aggregate number. In short, it is very useful for reconciling conflicting sets of hierarchical data.

(g) Return.

A function that brings in the previous display exactly as it was last seen on the screen.

14. *Subprograms—Action Functions*

These routines generally insert an identifying number, or a series of identifying numbers, of subroutines into the "routines to be run" segment of the driving table. Control is then turned over to the executive system and these routines are implemented.

(a) Proceed.

This action function causes the display function previously requested to be executed. When all display functions are executed, control returns to the executive system.

(b) Return.

As above.

(c) Finish.

Returns control to the executive system which takes steps to save all necessary information and disconnect from the central system.

(d) Initialize.

This control point signals the operating system to bring in the initialization display which permits re-definition of the type of display system required.

(e) Sequence.

This control point brings on the next set of data and forms an identical display (where this is legal). The data is prenumbered in an arbitrary fashion to permit this sequencing.

(f) Specification.

This control point brings the specification display to the tube face. This display allows re-specification of the type of graph and type of data required for the user.

(g) Turn Page.

When there is too much alpha-numeric information for the device's tube surface this control point brings in the next page of information associated with a particular display.

These major components form the structure of the software built to drive the MDS. This software contains mechanisms by which all the goals identified in Appendix B can be accomplished. The structure has been used in other application areas on the same problem, and for different problems. Thus far it has proved to have enough generality to readily encompass these other areas. More work will be needed in other application areas and with other computers before this structure can be ascertained to be truly general purpose. At least the initial experience has been encouraging.

DETAILED OBSERVATIONS—DECISION-MAKING PROCESS WITH THE MANAGEMENT DECISION SYSTEM

IN THE TEXT, CHAPTERS 7 AND 8 presented some general observations of the new decision process at a macro and micro level and Chapter 9 then followed with an overview of findings. These chapters were based on detailed tape-recordings, observations, and interviews of the decision makers as they used the MDS in the decision-making process. Some of the more interesting sections of this protocol are discussed in the material that follows. The managers started from the same base as before and used the system to arrive at an answer which then became the plan governing operations for the next month.

The material has been summarized as an introduction to what follows. All of the discussion is arranged by the nine cells of the framework so that the impact is presented as clearly as possible. The schematic of this framework, originally discussed in Chapter 3, is reproduced in Exhibit D–1.

SUMMARY OF DETAILED OBSERVATIONS (A)

This section summarizes the impact the MDS had on the specifics of the managers' actual decision-making process. A discussion of the points raised here together with sections of the protocol of the managers as they were involved in the decision-making process is given in what follows. A reading of this abstracted data provides the flavor of the new decision-making environment and the managers' reaction

Framework for the Decision-Making Process

		Intelligence	*Design*	*Choice*
S T R U C T U R E D	Generation			
	Manipulation			
	Selection			
U N S T R U C T U R E D	Generation	1 Low*	4 Medium	7 High
	Manipulation	2 High	5 High	8 Low
	Selection	3 High	6 High	9 Low

* Expected impact of the Management Decision System.

to it. The section is arranged by the nine cells of the framework and is also organized to match the bottlenecks discussed in Chapter 4.

Cell 1. Intelligence/Generation

(a) Data were found to be missing from the files. This was discovered because the managers lengthened their planning horizon (from 7 months to a rolling 12 months) and because they looked at more data than before.

(b) Some initial confusion due to the users' disbelief that these data could be "actual" so soon after month end.

Cell 2. Intelligence/Manipulation

(a) MPM and MM worked together during the entire process. As a result, MM was more familiar with information.

(b) Models were reviewed rapidly in turn and then manipulation was done on each in enough depth to reach a decision on the presence of a problem.

(c) The managers found the system easy and flexible to use and expressed themselves as being surprised at its simplicity and power.

Cell 3. Intelligence/Selection

(a) The selection process was more of a joint decision than before and was efficiently arrived at. That is, there was little or no time spent in arguing whether or not something was a problem. The models that were recognized as problems were identified quite expeditiously by all present.

(b) Criteria for selection as a problem remained as varied as before. There was no initial progress made in quantifying these variables.

(c) Comprehension by the managers was very rapid, a response never taking more than 10 seconds. Graphical presentation was felt by the managers to be a significant, and to them unexpected, feature.

(d) Both the MM, PM and the MPM contributed their own informal information as justification for unusual data that appeared on the screen. In some 40% of these cases the explanation was unknown by the other managers.

Cell 4. Design/Generation

(a) Several different strategies were tried in looking for a solution to any one of the problems. That is, a number of alternatives were suggested and their implications evaluated.

(b) The managers participated actively in the solution process, interacting with each other and the system. They felt that depth of analysis, quality, and speed were all favorably affected by the system. In addition, one of the managers saw the device as improving communication between individuals and groups. This occurs, he felt, because the MDS allows the impact of a suggestion to be seen, and discussion can be centered on the implication of the facts, rather than arguing over what are the facts.

Cell 5. Design/Manipulation

(a) A number of solutions were tried for each problem. Each of these involved manipulation of the data and a new presentation on the screen.

Management Decision Systems

Cell 6. Design/Selection

(a) The design process was an active iterative one where the "selection" process in turn "generated" a new solution for "manipulation" and "selection." All significant design alternatives passed through this three-step process more than once.

(b) Again, the managers were active in suggesting and selecting alternatives.

Cell 7. Choice/Generation

(a) Unlike the former process there was more than one acceptable solution generated for many of the problems. On the average 70% of the models had more than one solution developed.

Cell 8. Choice/Manipulation

(a) Initially the MDS was too awkward to use for this process with the result that only simple comparisons were made. For example, the managers would have liked to superimpose one graph over another for comparison purposes. This sort of feature was not available. Manipulation took the form of simply recalling the previous graph or line (e.g., previous forecast and present forecast).

Cell 9. Choice/Selection

(a) The managers were present and equally informed during the selection process. This resulted in briefer more specific discussion as to the reasons for or against a specific alternative. The level of common understanding was much higher and agreement seemed to be reached effectively and efficiently.

DETAILED OBSERVATIONS (B)

The detailed observations are arranged here by the nine cells of the framework. In Chapter 7 they were discussed in terms of the time sequence model of the decision process. This model was built from the protocol and observation of the new decision process, and remained basically stable over the initial nine-month observation period as well as subsequent periods. For purposes of reference, it is given as Exhibits D–2 and D–3.

Cell 1. Intelligence/Generation

(a) "We don't have any data here (working forecast, production, and inventory for the last three months of the year). Why?—We should develop some so we can look further out. . . ."

EXHIBIT D–2

New Process—Decision-Making Cycle*

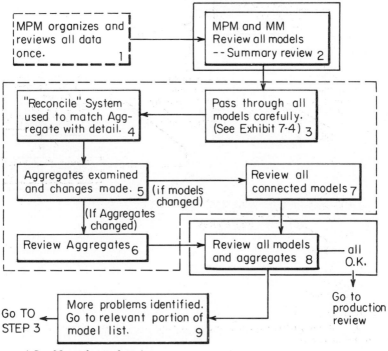

* See Notes for explanation.

NOTES: (Comments are keyed to box)

1. This process was employed by the MPM in sessions 1 and 2 but not thereafter. The manager indicated (see Appendix D) after the third session that he would no longer do this. Box 2 now became the first step.

2. No models are changed. This is a once-over-lightly review to find potential problems.

3. Each of the models is taken in turn and examined.

4. When the last model is finished, all models are compared with the relevant aggregate. No changes are made until step 7 is finished.

5. Step 3 repeated for aggregate.

6. 7. Depending on results of steps 4 and 5 one or both of the aggregates and various models are changed.

8. Models are then reviewed as in step 2.

9. If any problems are seen from step 8, then the process is iterated from step 3.

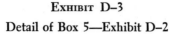

Exhibit D–3

Detail of Box 5—Exhibit D–2

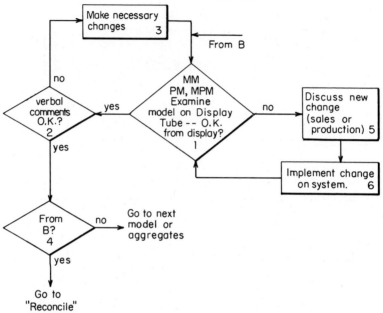

NOTES: D–3.

1. The information on the display system may or may not be acceptable to the managers.

2. If it is, they may remember some other factor which suggests a problem. This is discussed verbally.

3. If a problem is suspected, some change is made to the display and it is regenerated.

4. If there are no other factors and this is the first iteration, the next model in sequence is chosen. If this is not the first iteration, some other model or the reconcile process is dealt with next.

5. If the information on the display is not satisfactory, then a change is discussed.

6. This change is implemented on the display system.

The first time the system was used the MPM found that from 10% to 15% of the information was missing on each of the displays examined. With the display system this was very obvious, because the data-base contained zeros with the result that lines would level off or drop precipitously. This drew it sharply to his attention.

Identification of the fact that these data were missing resulted in the time being taken, there and then, to develop data for insertion into the files.

The reason for the missing data, according to the manager, was: "We don't normally look ahead that far (beyond 7 months) so we had not noticed it was missing. . . . Anyway we didn't have time to work with that much data. . . ."

(b) Entering the data for the latest period (e.g., February data on March 4th) took considerably longer than expected. That is, the process of entering actual performance data through the terminal was not fast. To insert the approximately 800 elements of data took something over three hours with two staff people involved.

(c) The first time the MM was exposed to the system his response was one of disbelief. After some confusion it transpired that it never crossed his mind that the system could contain "live" data for the preceding month so soon after the month end. By the time he saw the information, normally, it was from 10 to 12 working days into the month.

Cell 2. Intelligence/Manipulation

(a) After about 10 to 15 minutes of operation on the first "live" use of the system the MPM made the following statement: ". . . I have to get X—(MM) in to look at this performance with me. . . . I wonder what he is going to say about A–2, look at that Inventory. . . ."

Without there ever having been any mention of the possibility of the MM participating in this development process, except as a final review, the MPM suggested bringing him in. The MM was out of town at that point, so the first session was completed by the MPM alone. At the beginning of the next session the MM sat down with the MPM to go through the performance. They went through all models bringing each onto the screen— the entire process taking about 20 minutes. This was enough time to allow them to review all models. Both the MM, and MPM reacted to the situation reflected in each graph (see Exhibit D–3). Over time the process moved to the point where the PM was also involved.

(b) The initial pattern of activities thus far has been to pass through the aggregates and then all the models very rapidly without making any changes. The models are then passed through slowly with discussion on each. The ones identified as problems (i.e., where changes were made) were as in Table D–1.

TABLE D–1

Model Sequence Followed in Second Session

Step	Exhibit 2 Box Number	Models Examined
1	2	Review all models, Washers (W), Tumblers (T), Agitators (A), T–1, T–2, . . . T–N A–1, A–2, . . . A–N For a total of 30 models
2	3 & 4	Returned to models A–1 through A–N
3	3 & 4	Returned to models T–1 through T–N
4	5	T with models, A with models, W with T and A
5	7	A–1, A–2, A–4, A–9
6	8	As in step 1
7	3	Only T–3, A–1, A–4
8	5	As in step 4
9	7	A–1, A–2, A–8, T–3
10	8	As in step 1
11	3	Only A–1, A–4
12	5	As in step 4
13	7	A–1, A–2, A–4, A–8
14	8	As in step 1

On reaching each model, effort was spent determining if it was a problem. In each of the months observed in the experiment there was no overwhelming pattern of manipulation that was discernible. The manipulations that were used were simple and of the following types, the most frequently used listed first:

(1) Comparison of: Objective to Actual.
                     Exponential Forecast to Objective.
                     Production Plans and Total Inventory.
These would be emphasized by bringing them on and off the screen.

(2) Bring on last period's forecast.
(3) Bring on last year's actual sales data.
(4) Same data in noncumulative form.

These are all simple forms of manipulation, but at least three were done for each display. It is interesting to note that there were no changes of time spectrum (x axis) or rescaling during this stage.

The balance of the model list was dealt with in similar ways. One strategy that was used in the observation was the following: the simple assumption was made that the variable that looked suspicious was, in fact, normal. A temporary change was made so that it was displayed that way to see if any other variables were pushed too far off. For example, MM: "Give me 3 months' supply (looking at A–9) from July to October (makes change to display) . . . We can't do that, production (PM) will just laugh . . . Well, let's try. . . ." In this case, "months' supply" were changed to fall within the rule of thumb for all months until year's end. This change resulted in new production figures. These then became ridiculously high, by the managers' informal rules of thumb, and the model was classified as a problem.

This general sort of exploration process was used on all models that seemed to be questionable. It involved 3 to 6 manipulations per display, which in turn affected between 5 and 30 elements of information on the display.

(c) Some observations missing from the protocol are complaints in the early stages about awkwardness of use or similar comments expressing dissatisfaction with the system. The managers were able to specify the operations they wanted to perform and interpret the results. The error messages, when mistakes were made, were small in number. The users needed little prompting to find the correct procedure, but had some difficulty in combining procedures.

The keyboard and function-keys were awkward to use in their present location and an extra person was used to help at the keyboard.

Some simple user statistics in these groups of trials are given in Table D–2.

Cell 3. *Intelligence/Selection*

(a) Selection was a joint process—the managers agreed after discussion, but without any argument, that an area was a problem. For

TABLE D–2

Usᴇʀ Sᴛᴀᴛɪsᴛɪᴄs

Group	1	2	3
Control Points Missed	55	38	35
Incorrect or Unintended Action	29	17*	16*
Data Transmission Error*	30	26	21
Total Control Points Hit	575	450	375
Total Control Point Actions	380	290	210

* Largely due to hitting control-point too soon after previous action, a hardware problem.

example, MM: ". . . our inventory is way too low; we will have to increase production. . . . (changes production figure) . . . MPM . . . that is going to give you far too much production (that month). . . . Look at the reconcile display (this gives all production at the plant by month; calls for reconcile display) . . . PM . . . Yes, let's cut back on production for this."

Any suggestion by one member could be tested, immediately, by the other and problem areas mutually agreed to, there and then. At no point was there protracted or heated discussion on the identification of a problem. As the PM became more involved this selection became an even more iterative process.

(b) As was mentioned under (2), they did use different information at different times. For example: Model A–1 (looking at year-end position): MM . . . "Let's see what happened with last year's sales (adding the line to the graph). . . . We will be able to sell far more (this year) than the (exponential) forecast—that (exponential forecast, i.e., working forecast) has to be changed. . . ." Model B–1: MM ". . . That (year-end total) looks off. What did we predict last month (previous period's working forecast) . . . ? Hmm, well, if that's what we said then I don't see any point in changing this (this period's working forecast) now. . . ."

(c) Ease of understanding of the information portrayed seemed to be high. It was never more than 10 seconds, usually only 1 or 2, before either the MM, PM, or MPM had identified some feature of the display they felt was significant. For example, almost immediately after the display on Model B–2 appeared, MPM: "Look at our inventory position in July; we are going to have to make more in May and June to deal with that. . . . PM: We already have a heck of a lot of production scheduled. . . ." This nonstop stream of comments would come out as fast as their eyes could travel. Some form of light-pen action was taken within 30 seconds in every case of the Intelligence/Manipulation/Selection phases (except when extraneous subjects interrupted direct work on the problem—perhaps 10% of the time).

(d) At their first joint session the MPM arrived with the MM and they started work together. This was different from the old process where the MPM spent a lot of time (2 days) going through the data first by himself. When asked why (after the session) he no longer did this, he replied, ". . . I can understand the data by looking at the graph and there is no figure work we have to do now anyway. . . ." In other words, his comprehension from the graph was such that he did not have to go through the "immersion" process he used previously.

(e) The managers started from the top and worked down the list of models. As they worked through this list they seemed to follow the following kind of pattern. If a model was close to the objective and the "Months' Supply" (MOS) was at or near their rule-of-thumb for this figure, then no further exploration was made unless the managers remembered some other relevant fact not reflected in the information on the display (see below). Any model in this category, of course, might have to have its production schedule changed, but this was dealt with later (see 4, 5, and 6). Comments on these models, comprising some 20% of the total model list were typified by: ". . . Looks as if we are right on the mark all the way out to year-end (looking at exponential vs. objective) and we have enough inventory through June (the next quarter), in fact, the rest of the year looks O.K. . . . Not bad. . . ."

The pattern of recognition of "no-problem" was not always so straightforward. For example, MPM: "We are going to be way heavy on Inventory in June on B-4. . . ." MM: "No, that's O.K., a lot of that production is a special order for XYZ, Inc. We have a special deal with them for June for x units. . . . Let's see, if we take out x units (does so using key-board and light-pen), we should be O.K. . . . Yes, no problem; I mustn't forget to check with Z (regional marketing manager) on this. . . ."

In this instance, the obvious rule-of-thumb (three months of inventory) had been violated but they were able to identify a satisfactory explanation without any further manipulation. It is interesting that this identification took place in their minds, without any conscious search heuristics. It was an entirely informal process, relying upon the accumulated experience of the past months. When questioned afterwards, neither manager was able to identify other data sources he regarded as useful enough to formalize and let the machine have access to. In fact, they were not able to identify any other sources they might need. When reminded of the exchange quoted above the response was, "Yes . . . But these things come and go . . . It's too hard to keep track of them all."

Cell 4. Design/Generation

(a) On each problem there was more manipulation in the Intelligence phase under the MDS than under the former method (see 2). Similarly, the Design phase (steps 4, 5, and 6) was repeated more than once for each solution—more precisely, the complete protocol shows the following situation:

Number of Changes

		0	1	2	3	4	5	6	More than 7
Numbers of	prod.	–	1	2	11	10	5	1	–
Models changed	sales	–	3	6	8	8	4	1	–

"Changed" in this instance means that a number in either the sales plan (working forecast) or production plan was changed. For example, if the sales plan (working forecast) on model A-1 was changed once and never altered again, then it would appear under "1" above. However, if it was changed again, then there would be an entry under "2" instead.

To the extent that manipulation is an exploration of other possible solutions to a given problem, then it can be said that the problem becomes more sharply defined in the user's mind as manipulation is employed. Similarly, in the next major phase, Choice, the user not only has more than one solution to choose from, but also will have a more complete notion of the critical elements in the particular case.

(b) On the first occasion the MDS was used with "live" data, the MPM suggested the MM be brought in so they could work jointly. These combined sessions, right from the very beginning of the decision cycle, indicated a sharp shift from their previous work habits. The MM sat back at the end of the first joint session and said, "The depth of analysis we can now have should really make a difference to the kind of solutions we can get to this problem. . . . This thing (MDS) is going to let me analyze my problems in depth and a lot faster than our former method. . . ."

He went on, ". . . What we have to do now is bring the production people in here and we can all sit down with this thing (MDS) and get a decent job done . . . with them (Production Manager and staff) here we could get all the questions and problems ironed out in one sitting. . . ."

Without anyone's making the suggestion, the MM saw the device as a communications medium between the groups as well as a manipulative tool. By expressing ideas through the medium of the MDS the impact can be seen and discussion can be centered on the implications of the facts, rather than discussing what the facts are.

(c) After the first working session there was no noticeable tendency to deal with the short term, the next 5 months, in significantly greater detail than the rest of the year. That is, the managers modified and altered data at the end of the year as well as the middle. However, they always used a January to December time scale. There was no attempt made in this initial period to use a model year, July to June, or any other time period.

Cell 5. Design/Manipulation

(a) For each suspected problem area there were several iterations of steps 4, 5, and 6. The users tried changing all of the variables at one point or another, but the identifiable major patterns were in the following areas:

(1) Cutting or adding production in various months.
(2) Changing expected sales patterns.
(3) Altering the yearly totals and levels of sales and production.
(4) Moving emphasis from one model to another.

These were not tried in any particular sequence. The general approach was to proceed through steps 5 and 6 when someone suggested a change—if it resulted in an unacceptable solution, then they returned to step 4. If it was acceptable (violated no constraints) and they had no other acceptable solution, they returned to step 4 (Design/Generation); otherwise, they moved to the Choice phase. A typical sequence on this was, ". . . that looks O.K., but let's try a little less production too. . . ."

(b) The amount of manipulation was high in terms of sheer numbers —that is, the range of manipulation among the sessions varied from:

MDS

Low:	400 light-pen interrupts	5,000 numbers changed
High:	500 light-pen interrupts	7,500 numbers changed

Old System

_____ 2,000 numbers changed

The only significance such a statistic has is to point out that the volume of manipulation is high, and under the MDS it is sufficiently great that it could not reasonably be done under any other system. This quantity of processing was done in approximately three hours with the MDS.

(c) All of the control-point options were used during the sessions —during the first two sessions there were no suggestions for modification of the manipulation that was relevant to the immediate problem. However, many suggestions were later made for extensions to the system.

The most commonly used control points, other than trivial ones (such as proceed), were as follows:

Change Points	24%
End-Point Project	21%
Ratio	17%
+ or − Line	12%
All Other	26%

40% of the control points used involved multiple action commands; that is, from one request of the user a series of numbers was recalculated.

Cell 6. Design/Selection

(a) With the other managers being present there was always immediate reaction from the other party on his impression of the results of an action. MPM: ". . . We don't have enough inventory here (September, Model A-9) and for the next two months. . . . We should increase production to give us some more. Let's ask for a 3-month supply and look at that . . . (generates new display)." PM: ". . . No, that won't work. . . . Let's look at all production scheduled for July (generates new display) . . . see, that puts us way over, maybe if we moved some A-10 to August we would be O.K. . . . Let's try that. . . ."

Thus if the other manager saw a potential problem, there was immediate investigation. This trail of interacting models, where a change in one could logically affect another, could carry through two or three models. When a satisfactory stopping point was reached, they would pause and regroup—essentially starting back at step 4, from where they were. This interaction between models (i.e., increased sales of one model affected sales of one or more other models) was one of the factors making the managers' job so difficult. The MDS was used by the managers in visualizing this interaction as an aid in their understanding of the task.

(b) These steps 4, 5, and 6 were clearly iterative and the protocol shows that not a single design alternative passed through this three-step process only once. An exception was for trivial problems such as a minor model, A-14, with only a few hundred in inventory and a plan required for disposing of them. This was arrived at in one simple decision, namely to sell all of them next month to Distributor X whom they felt could be persuaded to buy them.

However, for more complex problems the three phases were repeated at least once, in many cases (50%) more than three times (See Design/Generation).

(c) There was no indication of anything more than a two-way comparison at each point. That is, one solution would be tried and compared with the previous state. If it looked better, it was saved (the insert option) and another solution tested. These two were then compared and a decision made as to whether it was acceptable, and so on. Thus it was always a two-way comparison and there was no attempt to try and compare, say, three sets. The system allowed the user to save a total of three sets of data. For example, one sales plan might concentrate on merchandising at the end of the year and another plan for a boost in sales at the middle of the year. These two typical plans might be displayed by the managers one after the other on the screen. They did not then display a third plan with yet another course of action. Instead, they would select one of the first two as the more desirable, perhaps modify it further, and make another comparison. They always dealt with two at a time in this initial one-year period.

Cell 7. Choice/Generation

As a result of the managers' reaction to the Design phase with the MDS they had available more than one solution. For example, the information in Table D-3 was built from the protocol and observation from the average of this group of sessions.

TABLE D–3

NUMBER OF MODELS WITH ACCEPTABLE SOLUTIONS

7 models had 1 acceptable solution developed
12 models had 2 acceptable solutions developed
5 models had 3 acceptable solutions developed
6 models had 4 acceptable solutions developed

That is, 23 models had more than one acceptable solution developed for them.

An example of such development was given in the previous three steps (4, 5, and 6) but is typified by the following exchange: MM: ". . . What would this (Model A-4, production change) look like if we did this (change September and October production instead of July and August) instead. . . ?"

He was, in essence, going back to steps 4 and 5 and trying out another possible solution.

Thus, there was generated more than one acceptable solution to many problems and this solution was carried through so that its impact on all relevant variables was visible to the manager.

Cell 8. Choice/Manipulation

There was only one form of manipulation visible; this simply was a regeneration of the previous solution and a comparison between it and the latest solution. The system was weak on this function, so physically it was not a rapid process. The managers did not find it easy to use. For example, they changed production on A-1 for the entire last half of the year. To flip back to the previous production schedule involved respecifying the values—a 2- to 3-minute task. With sales, one could go back to the previous display in 5 seconds but not forward a *second* time without the respecification. The system was poorly designed in this respect, and it is not possible to conclude whether this form of manipulation would have been used extensively had it been available. The users made statements to the effect that they could remember the numbers they were worrying about between the two pictures.

Manipulation, using the device, was almost nonexistent in this subphase. The manipulation, however, did take place in the mind of the users. If the examples from the protocol are examined, then it becomes clear that the manipulation was internal to the user and a very casual process. That is, the managers made comparisons between two solutions on the basis of what they remembered from solution 1 to what they could see in front of them regarding solution 2. A possibly desirable feature of placing one solution on top of the other or some similar function was not available in the early version of this system.

On a typical problem the users were looking at a different model, for different time periods, and concerned with different variables. It was not possible to structure the MDS to deal with this on the initial implementation.

Cell 9. Choice/Selection

(a) The selection process involved all of the managers. The MPM did not make a series of decisions by himself and *then* review what he thought the problem areas were with the MM and PM. By the same token the MM could no longer suggest a "solution" without the MPM and PM being able to counter with the potential problems (if any).

For example, consider the following exchange:

MPM: "We are O.K. on this (looking at last month's sales) so we might as well go with the forecast (i.e., Exponential Forecast)."

MM: "No, wait a minute. I authorized 500 units on a special to Distributor Y who had some building contracts (i.e., furnishing complete kitchens to home builders) if these are out, we cut sales by 60%. . . . We are very low . . . still the present forecast should be O.K. for the next quarter anyway. . . ."

MPM: "No, now if we only sold 600 units not 1,100, that means we are very soft with this model. . . . Look, let's drop the forecast and see how it looks. . . ."

Or the following:

MM: ". . . We should stay with this (latest working sales forecast for a 4-month period from 90 days out) we can get the production out some way or other. . . ."

PM: ". . . Maybe we can, but look where we end up with the other one (pointing to the *previous* working forecast for sales). It's not worth pushing production on this (T-1) when we are not going to be too far off anyway. . . . We will need a lot of push on the line (production line) to get out the extra on T-3.

(b) The above discussion was typical in the sense that there was some discussion, always about specific data, or a specific month, on all models before a decision was reached. That is, the managers had at least one specific interchange before agreeing on a final plan. There was no model decision taken where this did not happen.

In the old process about 50% of the models were dismissed by the MPM with the remark, "This one is O.K." or some similar phrase.

The discussion under the MDS did not necessarily result in any action (see 1, 2, 3) but both parties did at least comment specifically on the model and its *expected* performance. For example:

MPM: "We're O.K. on A-1 just about an objective."
MM: "Yes, but look at this inventory position (pointing to November, 8 months away) we are going to have to watch that later. . . ."
MPM: "Let's hope things pick up. We don't want to have to change production on that. . . ."

Conclusions (C)

All the sessions were tape-recorded and for the first nine months they were transcribed. The patterns that were obvious from this process led to the conclusions discussed in the body of the text in Chapters 7, 8 and 9. It is not appropriate here to provide extensive reproduction of these protocols. Their general implications for the impact of the MDS approach should be fairly clear from the extracts given in this chapter.

What is needed, of course, is to get as much more experimental evidence as possible with different managers, in different settings working on a wide variety of problems. Then we will be able to make more general statements as to the impact of the MDS and support such statements with data drawn from a variety of settings. At best we have only one data point as a result of this experiment. The next step is to collect more evidence from other ongoing management settings so that we can begin to develop a base of experimental findings to support further advances in this area.

BIBLIOGRAPHY

1. Adams Associates, *Computer Display Review*. Boston, Mass., 1967.
2. Anshen, Melvin, "The Managers and the Black Box," *Harvard Business Review*, November-December 1960.
3. Anthony, Robert N., *Planning and Control Systems, A Framework for Analysis*. Division of Research, Graduate School of Business Administration, Harvard University, 1965.
4. Barnard, Chester I., *The Functions of the Executive*. Harvard University Press, 1938.
5. Blalock, Hubert M., Jr., *Casual Inferences in Nonexperimental Research*. University of North Carolina Press, 1964.
6. Blumenthal, Sherman C., *Management Information Systems: A Framework for Planning and Development*. Prentice-Hall, 1969.
7. Bolt, Beranek and Newman, Inc., *Telcomp—Private Line Computation Service*. Cambridge, Mass., February 1966.
8. Bruner, Jerome S., *Toward a Theory of Instruction*. The Belknap Press of Harvard University Press, 1966.
9. Burck, Gilbert, and the Editors of *Fortune, The Computer Age and Its Potential for Management*. Harper & Row, 1965.
10. Carroll, Donald C., *Implications of On-Line, Real-Time Systems for Managerial Decision-Making*. M.I.T. Working Paper 165–66, 1966.
11. Chapin, Ned, *An Introduction to Automatic Computers*. (Second Edition.) Van Nostrand, 1963.
12. Chasen, S. H., and R. N. Seitz, "On-Line Systems and Man-Computer Graphics," *Astronautics & Aeronautics*, April 1967.
13. Clarkson, G. P. E., *Portfolio Selection: A Simulation of Trust Investment*. Prentice-Hall, 1962.

14. Clarkson, G. P. E., and W. F. Pounds, *Theory and Method in the Exploration of Human Decision Behavior*. M.I.T. Working Paper 32–63, 1963.
15. Cleland, D. I., and W. R. King, *Systems, Organizations, Analysis, Management: A Book of Readings*. McGraw-Hill, 1969.
16. *Computers and Management: 1967 Leatherbee Lectures*. Harvard Business School, 1967.
17. Corbato, F. J., "Introduction and Overview of the MULTICS System," *Proceedings of the F. J. C. C.*, 1965, p. 185.
18. Critchlow, A. J., "Generalized Multiprocessing and Multiprogramming Systems," *Proceedings—Fall Joint Computer Conference*, 1963.
19. Dartmouth College, Computation Center, *BASIC Manual*, January 1966.
20. Dearden, John, "Can Management Information be Automated?" *Harvard Business Review*, March-April 1964, pp. 128–135.
21. Dearden, John, *Cost and Budget Analysis*. Prentice-Hall, 1964.
22. Dearden, John, "Myth of Real-Time Management Information," *Harvard Business Review*, May-June 1966.
23. Desmonde, William H., *Real-Time Data Processing Systems: Introductory Concepts*. Prentice-Hall, 1964.
24. Diebold, John, "ADP—The Still Sleeping Giant," *Harvard Business Review*, September-October 1964.
25. Dreyfus, Hubert L., *Alchemy and Artificial Intelligence*. The RAND Corporation, December 1965, P-3244.
26. Edwards, J. D., "On-Line Business Data Processing," *Datamation*, September 1965.
27. Emery, James C., *Organizational Planning and Control Systems*. The Macmillan Company, 1969.
28. Emery, James C., "The Planning Process and Its Formalization in Computer Models," *Second Congress on the Information System Sciences*. Spartan Books, 1965.
29. Evans, Marshall K., and L. R. Hague, "Master Plan for Information Systems," *Harvard Business Review*, January-February 1962.
30. Fano, R. M., *The MAC System: A Progress Report*. M.I.T. Project MAC, MAC-TR-12, 1964.
31. Feigenbaum, Edward A., and Julian Feldman, eds., *Computers and Thought, A Collection of Articles by Various Authors*. McGraw-Hill, 1963.
32. Flanagan, David L., and Oscar V. Hefner, "Surface Molding—New Tool for the Engineer," *Astronautics & Aeronautics*, April 1967.

33. Gibson, G. T., "Time-Sharing with the IBM System/360-Model 67," *Proceedings of the SJCC*, 1966, p. 61.

34. Glans, T. B., B. Grad, D. Holstein, W. E. Meyers, and R. N. Schmidt, *Management Systems*. Holt, Rinehart & Winston, 1968.

35. Greenberger, M., ed., *Management and the Computer of the Future*. The M.I.T. Press and John Wiley & Sons, 1962.

36. Head, Robert V., *Real-Time Business Systems*. Holt, Rinehart & Winston, 1964.

37. Howard, James H., *Electronic Information Displays for Management*. American Data Processing, Inc., 1966.

38. I.B.M., *Quicktran Users Guide*. Form C-28-6800-2, 1967.

39. Kaufman, Arnold, *The Science of Decision-Making*. McGraw-Hill, 1968.

40. Le Breton, Preston P., *Administrative Intelligence—Information Systems*. Houghton Mifflin, 1969.

41. Licklider, J. C. R., "Consoles for Man-Computer Interaction," *Proceedings of the IFIP Congress 65*. Spartan Books, Vol. II, 1966.

42. March, James G., and Herbert S. Simon, *Organizations*. John Wiley & Sons, 1958.

43. Martin, James, *Programming Real-Time Computer Systems*. Prentice-Hall, 1965.

44. Menkhaus, E. J., "Interloc: Control Where the Action Is," *Business Automation*, July 1966.

45. Miethaner, E. C., "On-Line Branch Banking," *Datamation*, April 1966.

46. Miller, Robert B., *Psychology for a Man-Machine Problem-Solving System*. IBM Technical Report, TR 00.1246, February 19, 1965.

47. Morton, Michael S. Scott, "Program Management and Interactive Management Decision Systems," M.I.T. Working Paper 436–70 (Sloan School of Management), January 1970.

48. Morton, Michael S. Scott, "Strategy for the Design and Evaluation of an Interactive Display System for Management Planning," M.I.T. Working Paper 439–70, 1970.

49. Morton, Michael S. Scott, "Terminal Costing for Better Decisions" (with Andrew McCosh), *Harvard Business Review*, May-June 1968.

50. Morton, Michael S. Scott, "The Impact of Interactive Visual Display Systems on the Management Planning Process" (with James Stephens), *Proceedings of the IFIP Congress 68* (Edinburgh, Scotland), August 1968.

50a. Morton, Michael S. Scott, "Computer-Driven Visual Display Devices—Their Impact on the Management Decision-Making Process," Doctoral Dissertation, Harvard Business School, 1967.

51. Myers, Charles A., ed., *The Impact of Computers on Management*. The M.I.T. Press, 1967.

52. Parkhill, Douglas F., *The Challenge of the Computer Utility*. Addison-Wesley, 1966.

53. Parslow, R. D., R. W. Prowse, and R. E. Green, eds., *Computer Graphics*. Plenum Press, 1969.

54. Polya, G., *How To Solve It, A New Aspect of Mathematical Method*. Doubleday & Company, 1957.

55. Poole, Harry H., *Fundamentals of Display Systems*. Spartan Books, 1966.

56. Pounds, W. F., "The Process of Problem Finding," M.I.T. Working Paper 145–65, 1965.

57. Prywes, N. S., *A Problem-Solving Facility*, Prepared for Department of the Navy, Office of Naval Research, Methodology Division, Washington 24, D.C., under Contract NOnr 551(48), 20 July 1965.

58. Prywes, N. S., *Associative Memory in Heuristic Problem Solving*. University of Pennsylvania, 1962.

59. Prywes, N. S., *A Storage and Retrieval System for Real-Time Problem Solving*. Prepared for Department of the Navy, Office of Naval Research, Methodology Division, under Contract NOnr 551(48), 1 June 1965.

60. Rappaport, Alfred, ed., *Information for Decision Making: Quantitative and Behavioral Dimensions*. Prentice-Hall, 1970.

61. Reagan, F. H., "Viewing the CRT Display Terminals," *Data Processing Magazine*, February 1967.

62. Ream, Norman J., "On-Line Management Information," *Datamation*, March 1964.

63. Rosenberg, Art, "Time-Sharing: A Status Report," *Datamation*, February 1966.

64. Sass, Margo, and William D. Wilkinson, eds., *Symposium on Computer Augmentation of Human Reasoning*. Spartan Books, 1965.

65. Schoderbek, P. P., ed., *Management Systems: A Book of Readings*. John Wiley & Sons, 1967.

66. Sherr, Allan L., *An Analysis of Time-Shared Computer Systems*. M.I.T. Research Monograph #36. The M.I.T. Press, 1967.

67. Shuford, Emir H., Jr., *A Computer-Based System for Aiding Decision Making*. Spartan Books, 1964, pp. 157–168.

68. Shultz, George P., and Thomas L. Whisler, eds., "Management Organization and the Computer," *Proceedings of a Seminar Sponsored by Graduate School of Business—University of Chicago and The McKinsey Foundation.* The Free Press, 1960.

69. Simon, Herbert A., *Administrative Behavior, A Study of Decision-Making Processes in Administration Organization.* The Macmillan Company, 1965.

70. Simon, Herbert A., "Elements of a Theory of Human Problem Solving," *Psychological Review,* Vol. 65, #3, May 1958.

71. Simon, Herbert A., *Models of Man Social and Rational.* John Wiley & Sons, 1957.

72. Simon, Herbert A., *The New Science of Management Decision.* Harper & Row, 1960.

73. Simon, Herbert A., *The Shape of Automation for Men and Management.* Harper & Row, 1965.

74. Simon Herbert A., Richard M. Cyert, and Donald B. Trow, "Observation of a Business Decision," *The Journal of Business,* 1956, pp. 237–248.

75. Solomon, Irving I., and Laurence O. Weingart, *Management Use of the Computer.* Harper & Row, 1966.

76. Sprague, Richard B., *Electronic Uses of On-Line Real-Time Computers.* Ronald Press, 1962.

77. Springer, C. H., R. E. Herlihy, and R. I. Beggs, *Advanced Methods and Models.* Richard D. Irwin, 1965.

78. Swets, John A., Judith R. Harris, Linda A. McElroy, and Harry Rudloe, "Computer-Aided Instruction in Perceptual Identification," *Behavioral Science,* March 1966.

79. Taube, Mortimer, *Computers and Common Sense, The Myth of Thinking Machines.* Columbia University Press, 1962.

80. Tregoe, Benjamin, and Charles H. Kepner, *The Rational Manager.* McGraw-Hill, 1965.

81. Vitz, Paul C., "Preference for Different Amounts of Visual Complexity," *Behavioral Science,* 1965.

82. Westinghouse Electric Corporation Case, taken from *The Impact of Systems and Computers on Management and on the Accountant,* by C. G. Edge, L. C. Roy, and P. J. Sandiford, The Society of Industrial and Cost Accountants of Canada, Hamilton, Ontario, Canada, May 1966.

83. Widener, W. Robert, "New Concepts of Running a Business," *Business Automation,* April 1966.

84. Wilson, Ira G., and Marthann E. Wilson, *Information, Computers, and System Design.* John Wiley & Sons, 1965.

85. Withington, Frederic C., *The Use of Computers in Business Organizations*. Addison-Wesley, 1966.
86. Zannetos, Zenon S., *Management Information Systems and the Management Process—New Directions*. M.I.T. Working Paper 243–67, 1967.
87. Zannetos, Zenon S., *Toward Intelligent Management Information Systems*. M.I.T. Working Paper 155–65, 1965.
88. Ziegler, James R., *Time-Sharing Data Processing Systems*. Prentice-Hall, 1967.